OFFICE BUILDING DESIGN

Architectural Record Series

Architectural Record Books:

Hospitals, Clinics and Health Centers

Motels, Hotels, Restaurants and Bars, 2/e

Campus Planning and Design

Interior Spaces Designed by Architects

Houses Architects Design for Themselves

Techniques of Successful Practice, 2/e

Office Building Design, 2/e

Apartments, Townhouses and Condominiums, 2/e

Great Houses for View Sites, Beach Sites, Sites in the Woods,
   Meadow Sites, Small Sites, Sloping Sites,
   Steep Sites, and Flat Sites

Other Architectural Record Series Books:

Ayers: Specifications: for Architecture, Engineering,
   and Construction

Feldman: Building Design for Maintainability

Heery: Time, Cost, and Architecture

Hopf: Designer's Guide to OSHA

Edited by Mildred F. Schmertz, AIA; Senior Editor, Architectural Record

OFFICE BUILDING DESIGN

Second Edition

McGraw-Hill Book Company

New York   St. Louis   San Francisco
Auckland   Düsseldorf   Johannesburg
Kuala Lumpur   London   Mexico
Montreal   New Delhi   Panama
Paris   São Paulo   Singapore
Sydney   Tokyo   Toronto

ÆR AN ARCHITECTURAL RECORD BOOK

CONTENTS:
LOW - AND MEDIUM-RISE
HIGH-RISE
HIGH-RISE
SELECTED

Library of Congress Cataloging in Publication Data

Schmertz, Mildred F comp.
  Office building design.

  "An Architectural record book."
  Articles previously published in the Architectural record.
  Originally published in 1961 under title: Office buildings.
  Includes index.
  1. Office buildings.   2. Skyscrapers.   I. Architectural
record.   II. Office buildings.   III. Title.
NA6230.033   1975   725'.23   74-34114
ISBN 0-07-002320-4

234567890 HDBP 78432109876

The editors for this book were Jeremy Robinson and Hugh S. Donlan. The designer was Alberto Bucchianeri.
It was set in Optima by University Graphics, Inc.
It was printed by Halliday Lithograph Corporation and bound by The Book Press.

In the last half decade in the United States there has been an immense addition of new office space to the existing supply. Since 1970, over 500 billion square feet of space has been started including 48.7 million square feet on Manhattan Island alone. At its best, this new working environment is more handsome, practical, comfortable, and technologically interesting than ever before.

Many of the new office buildings, whatever their size, type, and location, are more handsome because of heavier investment in site development and landscaping. Low- and medium-rise corporate headquarters built in suburban and rural areas within the past five years show an increasing respect for the land that surrounds them. Several included in this book have been partially concealed underground to reduce their visible bulk. In some cases large lakes have been created and acres of meadow and forest land preserved.

More sophisticated zoning regulations in major cities have freed architects from the repetitive ziggurat and upended matchbox forms that characterized office buildings of the fifties and sixties. Designers have been encouraged to develop more elegant and complex shapes. These zoning incentives or trade-offs have also inspired developers to provide public plazas, terraces, pools and fountains on their sites in exchange for permission to incorporate more square feet within higher structures. There is a growing

PREFACE

awareness on the part of architects, developers, and the public that all truly handsome environments consist of more than just beautiful buildings. The esthetic experience includes not only a response to the form, façade materials, and details of a building, but must extend also to the enjoyment of the ground level spaces it makes as it joins its neighbors within the cityscape. Further, it is becoming more widely understood that office buildings and their pedestrian paths and squares should include or relate to such places for public enjoyment as cinemas, theaters, exhibition spaces, shops, and restaurants.

The best of the new office buildings are more practical and convenient to work in than ever before because of sophisticated interior space programming and planning techniques. They are also more comfortable because of improvements in their heating, ventilating, and air-conditioning systems and their control of heat loss and gain through better types of thermal insulation, and solar heat-reducing glass.

There have been other technological advances as well. Architects and engineers continue to improve the design and detailing of glass curtain walls and a report on their progress is included in the high-rise office building technology section of this book. This section also contains a discussion of the thermal insulation for the exterior members of the John Hancock building and a report on new developments in advanced rigid-frame design.

Recent structural solutions for the problems of wind loads in high-rise towers herald a new visual esthetic which is already taking form by the nation's most gifted architects. As these towers rise higher and higher, are constructed of lighter but stronger materials and lack the deadweight of heavy masonry skins, wind loads become a problem. Fortunately, economical structural systems developed to resist wind have come a long way from the simple rigid-frames devised years ago for buildings of 20 stories or less. The bundled-tube and truss-tube systems for steel structures up to 140 stories, and the framed-tube, tube-in-tube and modular-tube systems for similarly tall concrete structures, are exciting forms, which have begun to dramatically alter city skylines across the nation. These new technological concepts are analyzed in the article "Optimizing the Structure of the Skyscraper" included in the high-rise office building technology section. All the articles in this section are the work of RECORD senior editor Robert E. Fischer.

All other articles, with the exception of the report on the Ford Foundation building by Jonathan Barnett, were written by staff members of the RECORD, under the direction of editor Walter F. Wagner.

Cost figures included are applicable for the years in which the various buildings were completed. The cost figures given for the Hoffmann-La Roche building are for 1967. Alza Corporation, Ward Plaza and Western States Bankcard Association costs were for 1970. The sale prices given for the units in the Nagakin Capsule Tower in Tokyo are for 1971, and the construction cost figures for S.S. Kresge, Burroughs Corporation, the Federal Reserve Bank of Minneapolis, and Doubleday & Co. are for 1972.

Mildred F. Schmertz, AIA

LOW - AND MEDIUM-RISE OFFICE BUILDINGS

The 28 buildings for work which follow are among the best of those designed by U.S. and Canadian architects and completed in the past five years. Each was designed to relate as well as possible to its immediate environment. Many occupy 40-60-acre rural tracts selected for their natural beauty, others enhance industrial parks, while some take their place modestly on ordinary suburban or city streets. One of the most significant—the AIA headquarters building in Washington, D.C. (pages 25–34)—has been carefully designed to preserve the historic and beautiful Octagon and its garden.

All the buildings shown have been conceived as more than just comfortable and efficient places to carry on business. In every case the client has wanted a fine building to enhance its image—corporate or professional—and in most cases has been willing to pay for real amenities to be shared by workers and visitors alike. Only recently have so many low-density business buildings been designed in the United States to include broad terraces, richly landscaped courtyards and man-made lakes.

Although there has been more technical innovation in the design of high-rise structures (pages 166–192), low-rise buildings of structural and mechanical interest include those for Burlington (pages 2–5) S.S. Kresge (12–15), Noxell (pages 38–39), Hoffmann-La Roche (pages 45–50), Boots (pages 57–63) and Burroughs-Wellcome (79–84).

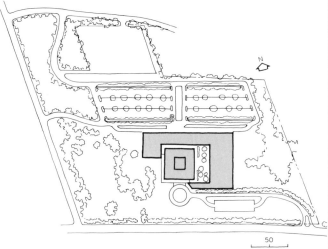

BURLINGTON CORPORATE HEADQUARTERS, Greensboro, North Carolina. Owner: *Burlington Industries, Inc.* Architects and engineers: *Odell Associates Inc.* Interior design: *Odell Associates Inc.* Landscape architects: *Odell Associates Inc.* General contractor: *Daniel Construction Company.*

This handsome corporate headquarters complex for the world's largest textile manufacturer unites in one location its various divisions, formerly scattered around Greensboro, North Carolina. The site for the new complex, a 34-acre former estate, is within that city's limits and near its downtown, but it has all the advantages of a more suburban location. The principal requirements given the architects were to design a building that would project the company's image and would provide flexibility and expandability for its future needs. The resulting building is actually two structures, separate but joined by bridges at three points. The six-story tower houses executive and personnel offices; a two-story (plus one floor below grade) building which surrounds the tower on three sides, contains divisional offices, meeting rooms and cafeteria. The most dramatic

feature of the complex is the exposed steel frame of the tower with its six-story-high trusses. Within this frame, reflective glass walls—170 feet wide on each face—mirror the huge trusses in a pattern that appears to double their number. The frame achieves a four-hour fire rating by virtue of a seven-foot separation from the walls of the building, and the installation of a ring of sprinklers in the soffit offers protection from heat build-up due to possible upward radiation of flames. All exposed steel is shop-painted with a long-life coating except for the roof grid frame which is of weathering steel. The low building also uses reflective glass for its bands of windows, combining this with plate steel spandrels and fascia. The entire design is based on a five-foot module: this is used for the structure, the integrated lighting pattern, air conditioning and heating distribution and controls, power and communications facilities, partitions, and built-in and movable furnishings. The buildings were constructed in 20 months on a CPM schedule, with design, fabrication of steel components and actual construction paralleling each other.

Gordon H. Schenck, Jr. photos

The entrance road circles a large fountain with a 70 foot diameter pool and jets that go up to 35 feet. The tower building is entered through a richly landscaped and terraced court between the tower and the low building. Three bridges connect the buildings.

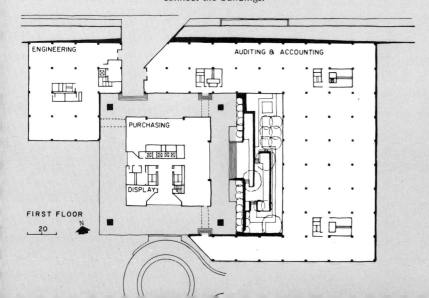

ENGINEERING

AUDITING & ACCOUNTING

PURCHASING

DISPLAY

FIRST FLOOR

20

N

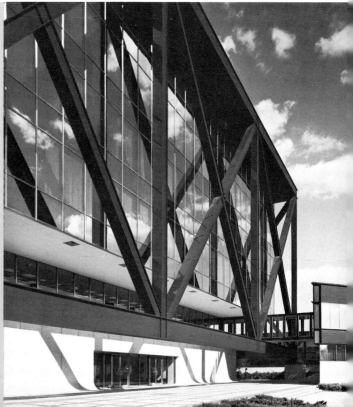

FIFTH FLOOR

EXECUTIVE OFFICES

Burlington made its move to a suburban location in part to provide its 1,000 employees with more pleasant surroundings. The expansive site and the delightful entrance courtyard with its intriguing sculpture, "Mayo," by Irish sculptor Robert Costelloe, provide open space on two scales. Ample parking, for visitors at the front, for employees at the rear, is provided. Interiors are pleasant in their own way,

CAFETERIA TRAINING CLASSROOMS

PERSONNEL DATA CONTROL OFFICES

SECOND FLOOR

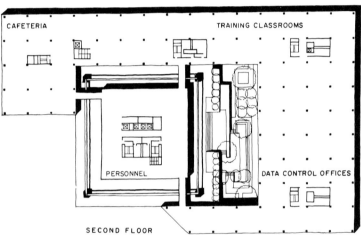

enhanced by works of art in various media: paintings, banners, prints are used in reception areas (top right), cafeteria (center), and in offices. In the tower, all vertical transportation is centralized in a 60-foot core, with open stairs for between-floor communication (shown at right, below).

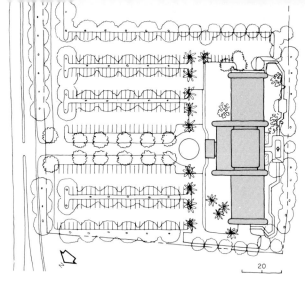

20

HOME OFFICE FOR CALIFORNIA CASUALTY INSURANCE GROUP, San Mateo, California. Owner: *California Casualty Indemnity Exchange.* Architects: *John Carl Warnecke and Associates, John Carl Warnecke,* director of design; *Carl Russell,* partner in charge; *Ronald Rossi,* project architect. Engineers: *Wildman and Morris,* structural; *Ralph E. Phillips, Inc.,* mechanical/electrical. Landscape architect: *Michael Painter.* General contractor: *Cahill Construction Co.*

Prompted by the need for more space and greater flexibility in its use, and by the desire to improve its employees' working conditions, California Casualty moved to a suburban location from its downtown San Francisco offices. Its new facilities not only meet those essential needs but provide rental space into which the company can eventually expand. The site is rectangular in shape, one long side fronting on a major thoroughfare, the other opening onto a golf course of unusual natural beauty. By making the building rectangular also, and by placing it at the rear of the site, parking was provided at the front, convenient to the street entrance. More important to the building's occupants, it preserved unimpeded the views to the golf course. The rear of the building's center portion

is quite open, especially at the second floor where the dining area is located. From this level, stairs lead to the landscaped sitting area adjacent to the golf course. Since there is a six per cent slope to the site, the garden area is slightly higher than the entrance lobby, to which it is connected by a corridor. The building was initially envisioned by the owners as almost twice as large as it ended up being. The original design premises, however, were found to be valid when the sizes were proportionally reduced. The rounded towers or "pods" which break the building length into thirds, were retained even though the smaller floor area did not require so many support facilities (contained in these towers), since they repeat on the front a design element important on the rear, and they provide interesting variations in office space. Large open spaces for office use, with central corridors, proved the simplest and most effective way of providing for the company's needs and for rental space. Executive offices on the fourth floor include a balcony in the rear center portion, sheltering the dining terrace.

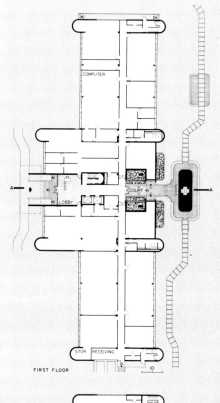

FIRST FLOOR

Robert Brandeis photos

SECOND FLOOR

Broad stairs and a series of terraces lead from the second floor dining room and its terrace to the informally landscaped sitting area, a pleasant place for noontime relaxation. The building exterior is buff colored concrete with deep vertical ribs, and anodized aluminum spandrels. At night strip lights under each spandrel emphasize horizontality.

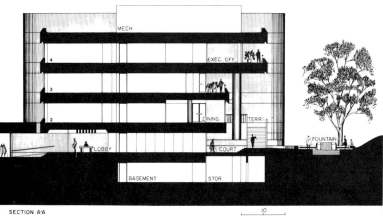

SECTION A-A   10

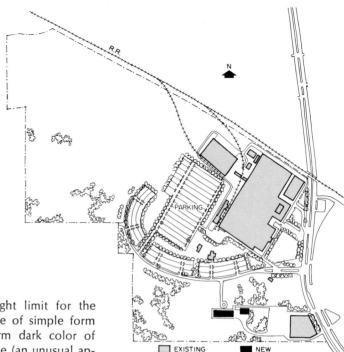

ENVIRONMENTAL SYSTEMS BUILDING, EMERSON ELECTRIC COMPANY, St. Louis, Missouri. Architects: *Hellmuth, Obata & Kassabaum, Inc.—Gyo Obata, principal in charge of design.* Engineers: *LeMessurier Associates, Inc.,* structural, foundation, soils; *HOK Associates, Inc.,* mechanical/electrical; *Bolt, Beranek & Newman, Inc.,* acoustical; *Seymour Evans Associates, Inc.,* lighting. Interior design: *Hellmuth, Obata & Kassabaum, Inc.* Graphics: *HOK Associates, Inc.* Rotunda display: *Obata Design, Inc.* Landscape architects: *HOK Associates.*

The environmental systems building is the first structure in the implementation of the master plan for development of the extensive Emerson Electric Company "park" on the outskirts of St. Louis. It is a multifunction building, in itself a working demonstration of many of the company's products. Included in its facilities are laboratories for product research, workshops to which architects and engineers can come for tests of mechanical and electrical designs, displays of products, and specially designed places for presentation of programs on lighting and air distribution to professionals.

The building in which all this takes place is a six-story (height limit for the area) rectangular structure of simple form but rich effect. The warm dark color of the weathering steel frame (an unusual application of the material) and spandrels, complemented by the gold reflective glass walls, the precise detailing and the elegant proportions, contribute to this effect. The main entrance is at grade but on the third floor of the building: the first two floors, containing laboratories and workshops are below grade. Besides the lobby on this floor, there are other public facilities, including the unusual Rotunda display, a multi-media means of demonstrating, teaching and analyzing lighting conditions which can be extended to provide actual experience of particular light effects; the cafeteria; and exhibits of the company's products in the field of interior climate design. The fourth and fifth floors each contain general offices for a company division, and are planned to meet two kinds of space needs: conventional, for which floor-to-ceiling movable partitions provide enclosed space; and open with modular furnishings. Work locations were set by computer survey.

Since the company's products are so closely related to the building field, the building naturally uses its products extensively both inside and out. Outside, special installations demonstrate electrical means to comfort and safety: brick terraces, walks and patios are kept snow- and ice-free; incandescent and mercury vapor fixtures, recessed in the ground, installed in overhang and in bollards, or pole-mounted, illuminate the building and nearby trees, as well as driving, parking and pedestrian ways.

EXISTING   NEW

George Cserna photos

3/8" WEATHERING STEEL PLATE

FOAMED IN PLACE INSUL.

2-HR FIREPROOF'G

SPRAYED ON FIREPROOF'G

1" INSUL. REFLECTIVE GLASS

1" WEATHERING STEEL PLATE

3'-6" SPANDREL

10'-2" WINDOW

4'-10 1/2"

4'-8 3/4"

The exposed steel frame (left) is of weathering steel, an unusual application of the material, chosen for both its warm color and its industrial look. Separation of the columns from the curtain wall achieves the required fire rating. Weathering steel spandrels and reflective glass—gold, to complement the steel color—make up the curtain wall. All surface temperatures on glass,, walls, floors, etc., are kept at a minimum 55 deg level in winter so work stations next to glass are comfortable. The cooling load in summer was found to be reduced by use of the reflective glass. The lobby (top right) is at grade but is actually on the building's third floor, as is the cafeteria (center). Lighting in these spaces uses company products and ceiling systems. General office areas (bottom right) are open-planned for use of a system of movable modular furnishings.

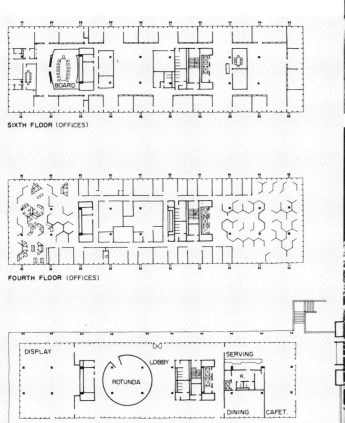

SIXTH FLOOR (OFFICES)

FOURTH FLOOR (OFFICES)

DISPLAY

LOBBY

ROTUNDA

SERVING

K

DINING   CAFET.

THIRD FLOOR

20

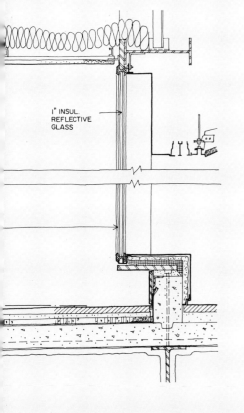

1" INSUL. REFLECTIVE GLASS

S. S. KRESGE COMPANY INTERNA-
TIONAL HEADQUARTERS, Troy,
Michigan. Architects-Engineers-Plan-
ners: *Smith, Hinchman & Grylls Asso-
ciates, Inc.*—project manager: *William
R. Jarratt*; project designer: *Charles T.
Harris.* Landscape architects: *Johnson,
Johnson & Roy, Inc.* Construction
managers: *Darin & Armstrong, Inc.*

This corporate headquarters on a
30-acre site in suburban Detroit
houses a staff in excess of 2000
persons, engaged in the operations
of one of the world's largest re-
tailers: S. S. Kresge Company.

Both client preference and
local zoning ordinances dictated a
low, horizontal complex, with the
client further stipulating these
three design criteria: areas of large
contiguous but flexible space for
certain multi-employee operations; other areas to contain a
maximum of exterior wall for
various-sized private offices; and
both types of space to allow for
rapid and economic future expansion without dislocation of normal
business activities.

The basic design decision of
Smith, Hinchman & Grylls was the
creation of a steel-framed modular
building located diagonally on the
site to soften the perimeter masses
as they relate to the adjacent major
traffic arteries (see site plan).

The complex consists of 13
modules (each 100 by 100 feet)
from two to four stories high, as
function dictated, containing just
over 10,000 square foot per floor.
Total cost of the 500,000 (gross)
square foot building was $27 mil-
lion or approximately $40 per
square foot.

Each module is serviced by a
core tower containing stairs, elevators, utilities and mechanical
equipment. Where maximum wall
exposure is required for offices,
modules are connected at their
corners, creating interior courts
such as the one shown on the opposite page, lower right. Where
large, uninterrupted spaces are
needed, modules are connected at
their faces; future modules, with
their own core towers, can be
added easily to existing units.

Because of the suburban nature of the site, the architects decided on a weathering steel curtain
wall, bronze-tinted glass and
complementary masonry block
units, all of which would blend
harmoniously with the setting. The
masonry block on the service
towers is specially-sized (10 by 16
in.) silo brick, in a brown glaze.

The choice of weathering steel for the curtain wall (section shown below) was made for consistency with the steel-framing of the structure.

In developing the design of the curtain wall—first of its type constructed anywhere—the architects prepared performance-type contract documents for profile, finish and performance criteria only; fabrication and assembly methods were left to the discretion of the contractor/bidder.

Rather than conventional assembly from welded bar stock, the selected system employed extruded steel shapes that eliminated exposed continuous welds and permitted better outside drainage.

Not only do the extruded members remain straight and free of twist, but economy resulted from elimination of miles of continuous welding. Weight reduction also resulted.

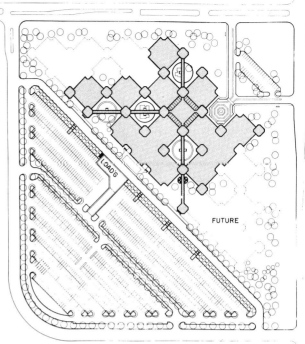

FUTURE

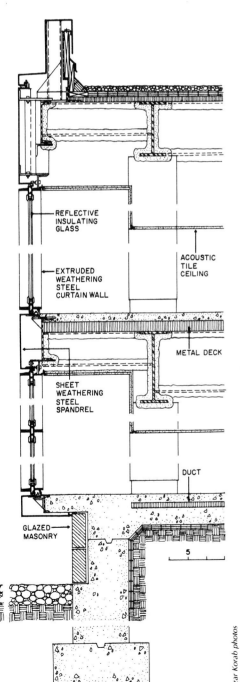

REFLECTIVE INSULATING GLASS

ACOUSTIC TILE CEILING

EXTRUDED WEATHERING STEEL CURTAIN WALL

METAL DECK

SHEET WEATHERING STEEL SPANDREL

DUCT

GLAZED MASONRY

5

Balthazar Korab photos

The towers are not structurally integrated with the modules. In the site plan, notches in the modules, evident at the corners, indicate where towers would be constructed for expansion. This would occur primarily to the north.

By nature, the business of this company entails two functions that are well-expressed in the building: accounting and buying.

The vast accounting operations and computer facilities occupy the large open spaces created by blending several modules. These spaces are shown in the lower right portion of the plans.

The other function expressed in the building—the buying operation—involves thousands of visitors or vendors who call on the middle management persons occupying the offices in the single modules.

Circulation to all these areas is accomplished by a series of diagonal pedestrian corridors emanating from the multi-storied lobby (far right), commodiously planned to accommodate the large numbers of daily visitors. The sky-lighted lobby is actually· another courtyard, providing vistas for offices on several levels.

The pedestrian routes go off, connecting all units on the first and second levels, traversing the landscaped courts (see plans and photo, center).

All vertical circulation in the building is confined to the towers. To encourage the use of stairs and reduce elevator loads, entry to the building is on the second level. This means that in a three-story module, only one flight of stairs must be climbed or descended to reach the next level. Main elevator use is in reaching the fourth-floor executive offices.

Employee entrances are conveniently located near the parking lot and by pedestrian linkages.

Besides office space, the building houses a cafeteria seating 600 persons, meeting rooms (below), employee lounges, a printing plant and specially-detailed executive offices (top).

Smith, Hinchman & Grylls provided complete architectural and engineering services for this project, in addition to designing the interiors and developing a graphics program for the complex. Landscaping, the largest single private contract let to date in Michigan, was designed by a division of the architects' office. The landscaping features large expanses of lawn and ground cover.

Although the framing of the modules was of conventional column and beam in structural steel, the four-story lobby has its roof carried on a two-way Vierendeel space frame supported on eight columns. This design, combined with the sky-lighted roof area, provides a feeling of openness and a view for some of the offices of the activity generated by numerous daily visitors.

Like all entries to the building, the lobby is at the second level, with easy access by one flight of stairs to ground floor and third floor offices. Elevators go to the fourth-floor executive offices.

Leading from the lobby, pedestrian concourses cut across the modules at ground and second levels.

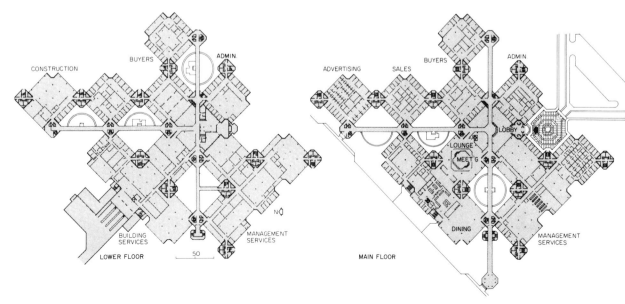

LOWER FLOOR

MAIN FLOOR

E. R. SQUIBB & SONS, INC. WORLD-
WIDE HEADQUARTERS, Lawrence-
ville, New Jersey. Architects: *Hell-
muth, Obata & Kassabaum, Inc.—*
principal-in-charge of design: Gyo
Obata; principal-in-charge: Jerome J.
Sincoff; master planning/program:
George Hagee; project designer:
David Suttle; interior designer: Mi-
chael Willis; graphic design: Charles P.
Reay; lighting: Eugene H. Fleming III;
construction administrator: William J.
Harris. Landscape architects: *The Of-*
fice of Dan Kiley. Engineers: *LeMes-*
surier Associates, Inc. (structural);
Golder, Gass Associates, Inc. (soils);
Joseph R. Loring & Associates (me-
chanical/electrical). Consultants: *Mc-*
Kee-Berger-Mansueto, Inc. (cost); *Flam-*
bert & Flambert, Inc. (food service);
Earl L. Walls Associates (laboratory).
Contractor: *Huber, Hunt & Nichols.*

Sited in gently rolling New Jersey
countryside, this combined headquarters and research facility by
Hellmuth, Obata & Kassabaum for
the E. R. Squibb & Sons pharma-
ceutical firm comprises seven
buildings, linked by a glassed-in
pedestrian spine. Each building is
one or more square (90 by 90 feet)
modules joined by service cores
containing stairs, elevators, restrooms and utilities. Maximum
height is four stories.

The design solution provides
maximum lateral expansion flexibility—an inherent quality of the
modular approach—in a suburban
context where land is available.
But this is not the only advantage
in breaking office space down into
smaller, arrangeable units. Another is the obvious ease with
which personnel and departments
can be grouped in neighboring
modules.

Since the modules themselves
house just the office and research
spaces, services and amenities for
employees were located in a central building containing: a 662-
seat restaurant and cafeteria overlooking the lake; a medical center;
a store; and an art gallery.

Once into the complex, orientation and directions are provided by a color-coded graphics
system that also adds accent to the
essentially all-white halls and secretarial areas.

In each office module, uphol-
stery, columns and accessories are
painted the same accent color
throughout. The color changes
from module to module horizontally, but remains vertically constant within any module. A reverse
system is used in the research units.

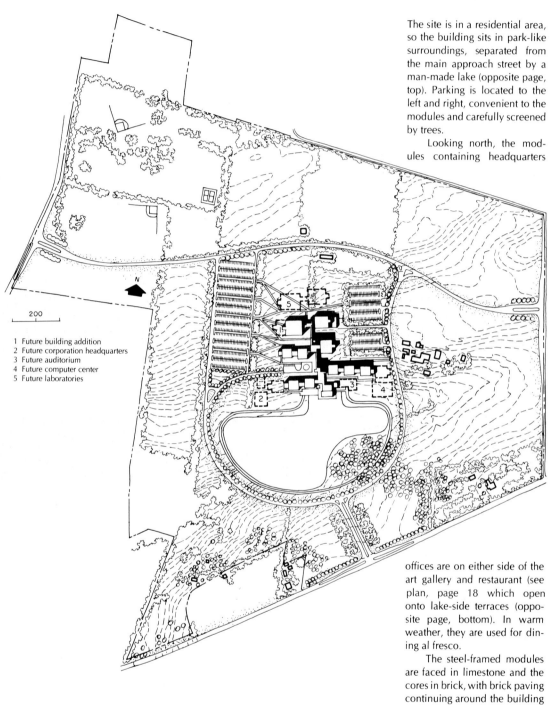

1 Future building addition
2 Future corporation headquarters
3 Future auditorium
4 Future computer center
5 Future laboratories

The site is in a residential area,
so the building sits in park-like
surroundings, separated from
the main approach street by a
man-made lake (opposite page,
top). Parking is located to the
left and right, convenient to the
modules and carefully screened
by trees.

Looking north, the mod-
ules containing headquarters

offices are on either side of the
art gallery and restaurant (see
plan, page 18 which open
onto lake-side terraces (opposite page, bottom). In warm
weather, they are used for dining al fresco.

The steel-framed modules
are faced in limestone and the
cores in brick, with brick paving
continuing around the building
and into the main lobby. Bronze
glass is used, with dark bronze
mullions.

Future expansion—offices,
laboratories, computer facilities
and auditorium—is designated
on the site plan by the num-
bered, outlined areas (legend).

Alexandre Georges

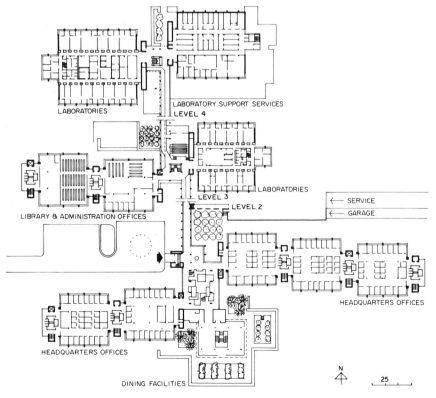

LABORATORIES

LABORATORY SUPPORT SERVICES
LEVEL 4

LABORATORIES
LEVEL 3

LIBRARY & ADMINISTRATION OFFICES

LEVEL 2

← SERVICE
← GARAGE

HEADQUARTERS OFFICES

HEADQUARTERS OFFICES

DINING FACILITIES

N

25

The architects changed from steel framing to poured-in-place concrete for the service building housing the restaurant (photos opposite) primarily to change the architectural environment from the sleek, efficient working areas. In keeping with the intent, lighting was changed from fluorescent to incandescent, and the concrete was sprayed with a textured surface for both warmth and sound-absorption.

Since the ceiling is also a landscaped plaza above, the waffle-slab provides extra support, while being attractive to

see in the rooms below.

A middle-management office (opposite, top) measures 10 by 15 feet. All offices have a three-dimensional coffered ceiling system, and gray carpet. Ernst Haas color photographs (shown in the conference room above) and V'Soske-designed wall hangings are used throughout the offices.

The table in the conference room can be arranged in various configurations and the carpet continues up the walls and over the ceiling to meet the lighting unit, dropped slightly.

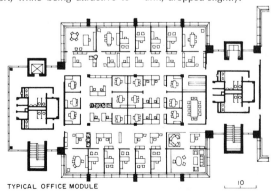

TYPICAL OFFICE MODULE

10

C. BREWER & CO., LTD. HILO OFFICE BUILDING, Hilo, Hawaii. Owner: C. Brewer & Co., Ltd. Architects for building design, interior design, furnishings and equipment: *Ossipoff, Snyder, Rowland & Goetz*. Engineers: *Shimazu, Shimabukuro & Fukuda, Inc.* (structural); *Robert Hamilton & Company* (mechanical); *Douglas MacMahon* (electrical). Landscaping: *George S. Walters & Associates*. Consultant: *Bruce Hopper* (graphics). General contractor: *Swinerton Hawaii Venture*.

The client wanted to house a computer facility and an agricultural office operation in a newly-developed part of Hilo, Hawaii. Formerly a manufacturing area, the site is a short peninsula in a backwater pond connected to Hilo Bay; parks surround the pond.

In every way suited to its environment, this office building relates to native architecture by simply being appropriate to the moist, semi-tropical climate and seaside location.

For instance, all materials are self-maintaining: corrugated metal roofing with embedded mineral; self-oxidizing natural steel; stained redwood decking; bronze glass and aluminum skin walls; and sandblasted concrete.

The ground floor is reinforced concrete and is earth-retaining. Because of the threat of tidal waves in the area, the ground floor is so designed that interior partitions and the exterior skin walls could fail without causing the structure to collapse.

Sun-screening and rain protection on all sides of the three-winged building are provided by a 6-foot roof overhang. Trees planted close to the offices reduce glare and direct sun into the building, eliminating need for any other sun shade devices.

Owing to the gentle slope of the site, the entry (interior right) is at the second floor or main level and open on both sides, forming a naturally-ventilated lanai, overlooking—as do all parts of the building—gardens of shade trees and azaleas.

Each office wing has a hipped roof, with a vinyl skylight in each plane (photo top right). Air handling equipment is located in the peaked portion of the roof, between trusses. Steel was selected for the long span needed to achieve the overhang and a light roof, and to minimize interior columns. Lightness prevails here.

Wayne Thom photos

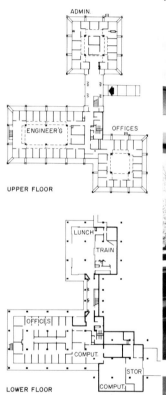

ADMIN.

ENGINEER'G

OFFICES

UPPER FLOOR

LUNCH

TRAIN

OFFICES

COMPUT.

STOR

COMPUT.

LOWER FLOOR

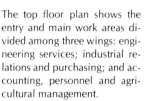

The top floor plan shows the entry and main work areas divided among three wings: engineering services; industrial relations and purchasing; and accounting, personnel and agricultural management.

The lower plan (ground floor) shows two wings housing computers and data processing, with a training room and lunch room that can be combined in the third wing.

Skylights admit natural light to the offices (right) and help define interior circulation. Hallways and doors are minimized. Each office has a built-in credenza facing the glass wall and the view of adjacent gardens, with water and mountains in the distance.

THE BURROUGHS CORPORATION
WORLD HEADQUARTERS, Detroit,
Michigan. Architects for building design, interior design and furnishings,
acoustics, lighting and landscaping:
Smith and Gardner. Engineer: *Robert
Darvas* (structural). Consultants: *Unimark Inc.* (graphics); *Michael Kenny*
(cost). Contractor: *Barton Malow Co.*

Desiring to keep its corporate
headquarters in Detroit's New
Center area—where this computer
builder has maintained operations
since 1904—the Burroughs Corporation hoped that new life might
be achieved for some of its aging
1914 factory buildings.

The architects' feasibility
study supported the idea, whereupon three reinforced concrete,
five-story loft buildings were selected for the new headquarters
complex. The remaining buildings
on the 20-acre site—18 manufacturing and storage buildings—
were demolished.

The saved buildings were
completely stripped of all exterior
walls, finishes, utilities, stairs—
down to the skeleton frame.

The three buildings were
linked centrally and at the ends by
new five-story core structures
housing stairs, elevators and utilities, and providing lobbies and
secondary entrances. A new canopy and foyer were added for the
main entrance.

To close in the skeletal structure, the architects designed precast concrete panels with limestone aggregate, measuring 19 feet
6 inches by 11 feet 6 inches. The
window panels, weighing approximately seven tons, hold two lights
of bronze glass separated by an
aluminum mullion. These 3½-
inch thick panels sheath the existing reinforced concrete frame,
each secured with bolted and
welded connections. Stainless
steel cap flashing was used.

On the ground floor, a curtain
wall was installed, consisting of
¼-inch clear float glass, 10 feet
high around the office area and
1-inch insulating glass around the
computer/display area. Where
privacy was desired, porcelain
steel panels were used.

The building comprises 675,-
000 gross sq ft of floor area, rehabilitated at a cost of $26.5 million
The architects claim structural
costs savings amounted to approximately $2.2 million.

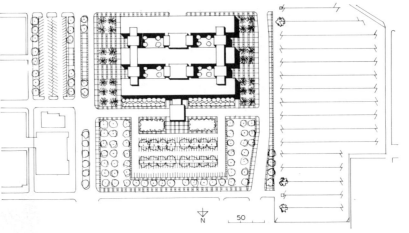

The canopy soffit shown right is paneled in 1½-inch deep, anodized aluminum pans suspended from the canopy with tapered teak dividing strips. Exposed aggregate paving and matched maple, locust and linden trees are the main ground elements. A luxurious entry features narrow-stile aluminum doors 10 feet high and 3 feet wide—52 of them throughout the building—in bronze anodized finish, and glazed with bronze glass. Parking for 1400 cars is provided nearby.

David Iordano photos

David Jordano photos

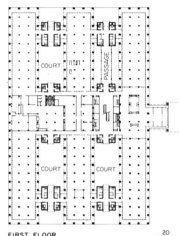

FIRST FLOOR   20

As the plan for a typical floor shows, each of the three structures is conveniently linked at three points. Elevators are located in the central core, with the end linkages containing stairs and restrooms. Open courts are formed by the walls of the buildings and the new ones made by the linkages.

The lobby (upper left) includes leather-covered seats on a sunken concrete base. All counters, drinking fountains, and table tops are Italian (Perlato) marble, 1½ inch thick.

The floor in the executive office (left) is quarry tile with matching grout. Vinyl asbestos tile is used, however, in most of the building. Drywall floor-to-ceiling partitioning is used throughout for sound control.

Ezra Stoller © ESTO photos

AIA NATIONAL HEADQUARTERS BUILDING, Washington, D.C. Architects: The
Architects Collaborative—principal-in-charge: Norman C. Fletcher; senior-associate-
in-charge: Howard F. Elkus; job captains: James F. Armstrong, John E. Wyman;
landscape designers: Knox C. Johnson, Hugh T. Kirkley; interiors: Ann G. Elwell;
architects' representative: Richard T. Malesardi. Engineers: LeMessurier Associates,
Inc. (structural); Cosentini Associates, Inc. (mechanical); Bolt, Beranek & Newman,
Inc. (acoustical); Golder, Gass Associates (soil). General contractor: The Volpe
Construction Company, Inc.

Ask an architect if a given handsome, historic, landmark building
and its garden should be preserved and he would say: "If at all
possible, yes." To the question as to whether one can design a
contemporary structure which would effectively blend with a no-
table building of bygone style, he would reply: "Certainly." If
pressed to recommend how this could best be done, he might very
well say: "Hold a competition!" Finally, if asked how best to make
sure that the competition winning scheme would respect the landmark and its neighborhood, he would add: "There should be a
disinterested board of review with power to accept or reject."

In the problems inherent in expanding their Washington
headquarters, the American Institute of Architects made three fun-
damental decisions—each of which reflect the foregoing beliefs
and aspirations of the typical architect, and a final decision reflecting the necessary pragmatism of the profession. First, they decided
to preserve the historic and beautiful Octagon and its garden;
second, they held a competition for the design of a new headquarters building to share the site and be in harmony with the
landmark; third, with some chagrin they deferred to a series of
rejections by Washington, D.C.'s Fine Arts Commission (which the
AIA helped create) of the winning design and modifications thereof;
fourth, they faced the necessity of accepting the resignation of the
competition winning firm and selected another architectural firm
by a method other than holding a formal competition.

The results would appear to be the very best that architects
designing for themselves can do. By living up to their own highest
standards and practicing what they preach, the architectural profession has not only enhanced the Washington landscape, but it
has created the physical framework for projecting a continuously
effective image for itself.

The 175 year-old Octagon occupies the corner of a triangular site at the juncture of New York Avenue and 18th Street in Washington, D.C. The garden at its rear has been rebuilt and is slightly larger than it was before the new headquarters building was wrapped around it. As the section and ground floor plan (right) and the sidewalk photo (below) indicate, a broad curving plaza forms a pedestrian path, open to the public, which connects the intersecting streets. The architects—Norman Fletcher and Howard Elkus of The Architects Collaborative—conceived the plaza as an extension of the garden, paved it in red brick to match the old brick in the reconstructed garden paths, and extended this brick into the ground floor exhibition space of the new structure. Conceived as a "background building," the new headquarters permits the Octagon House to dominate (left).

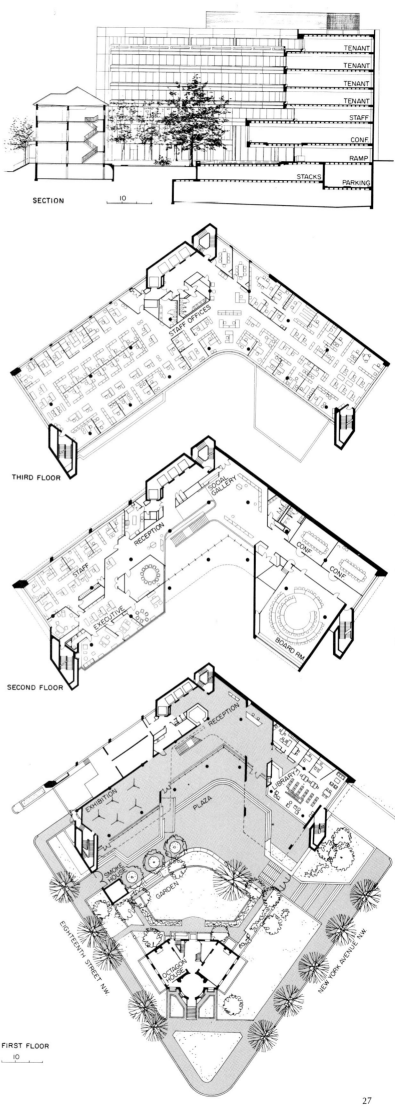

SECTION   10

THIRD FLOOR

SECOND FLOOR

FIRST FLOOR   10

To walk about the AIA's new headquarters is to sense that the building is correct, right, and designed as it should be. From the lobby mezzanine (left and above) one looks down into the ground floor exhibition space and across the plaza to the Octagon and its garden. Together the latter have become the focus of the composition, playing the same role in space that a fountain, or gazebo or pavilion does in the context of other scales. Because of skillful massing, the new building, in spite of its size, does not appear to crowd the landmark. At present the transition between the plaza and garden is gentle. As the new trees grow larger the integration of the two spaces will continue to improve. The generous exhibition gallery (below), in conjunction with the broad plaza affords the AIA the opportunity to mount combined indoor and outdoor displays to further the public interest in architecture and the environment. The prominent location of their headquarters, within a short walk from the White House, should bring many visitors to the AIA's exhibits, provided they are frequent, well done and well publicized.

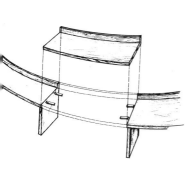

The offices of the president of the AIA (top left) and the executive vice president (bottom left) overlook the plaza and the Octagon garden. The spatial arrangement of the latter's office is particularly efficient and attractive because of the skillful way in which the room is divided into deskwork, conference and reading areas. The conference center (above) projects out over the plaza. It has been designed to accommodate a full range of audio-visual aids. The circular desks can be disassembled and rearranged or stored as shown in the detail (left). Open planning is used throughout the general offices and the system of partitioning consists of commercially available storage units surfaced in white laminated plastic (right).

The radial axes of Major Pierre L'Enfant's plan for Washington, D.C. shaped the non-rectangular corner which the Octagon House, designed in 1798 by William Thornton, turns so elegantly. One hundred and seventy five years later, architects Norman Fletcher and Howard Elkus of TAC have completed the composition.
The events which led to their commission to design the new AIA National Headquarters Building, and the considerations which influenced their final design were complex and difficult, but the results are distinguished.

The history of the project

In 1960, the AIA Committee on the Profession cited "the pressures of a growing membership and the increasing numbers of jobs to be done for the profession" as reasons for building a new national headquarters. The existing headquarters then included the Octagon House and an administration building beyond the garden which had been constructed in 1941 and incorporated the old stables on the site. A "New Headquarters Building Committee" was formed whose members were: Hugh A. Stubbins, Jr. FAIA, William L. Pereira, FAIA, and Arthur G. Odell, Jr., FAIA. Its chairman was Leon Chatelain, Jr. FAIA.

This committee decided that further vertical expansion of the administration wing was unfeasible from both a structural and architectural standpoint and that horizontal expansion would encroach upon the garden and call for extensive and costly additional land acquisition. After examining the possibility of moving the AIA headquarters out of Washington, the committee concluded that to be effective, politically and symbolically, the AIA headquarters should remain in the capital.

The committee, aided by the architectural firm of Satterlee and Smith, and with the help of a real estate consultant, examined the Octagon House site in terms of the prestige inherent in its proximity to the White House, the presence of a cherished landmark, and the economics of preserving and maintaining the latter. Research confirmed that the landmark would be hard to sell, but on the

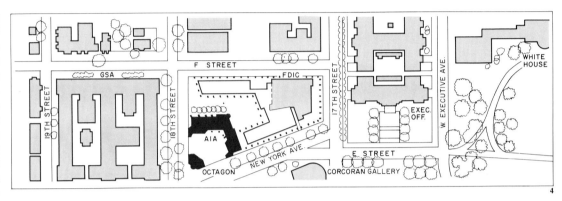

other hand, the land itself had an equity value of almost $1 million for building on the site. Other sites in Washington were studied from many standpoints. The advantages, however, continued to lie with the present site, even though preserving the Octagon House would make the design of the new headquarters more complicated and difficult. Not the least of the difficulties which could be foreseen was the fact that additions adjacent to the Octagon House, as a registered National Historic Landmark in an area of the District of Columbia over which the Fine Arts Commission has review authority, would be subject to approval by this body.

In 1963 the "New Headquarters Building Committee" was disbanded and a new group with a slightly different title was formed. The new members of the "New Headquarters Committee" were: Robert F. Hastings, FAIA, Henry L. Wright, FAIA, and chairman Charles M. Nes, Jr., FAIA. Stubbins and Chatelain continued to serve. Because the AIA membership had

voted that the architect for the new building should be selected by competition, late in 1963 a jury was selected. Stubbins agreed to serve along with Edward L. Barnes, FAIA, J. Roy Carroll, FAIA, O'Neil Ford, FAIA and John Carl Warnecke, FAIA.

The competition program charged the prospective competitors with ". . . the creation of a design for a new National Headquarters Building that will satisfy both physical and spiritual functions—a building of special architectural significance, establishing a symbol of the creative genius of our time yet complementing, protecting and preserving a cherished symbol of another time, the historic Octagon House."

Winners of the two-stage competition were Mitchell/Giurgola Associates. Their winning design (fig. 1), announced in November 1964, featured a semi-circular, concave glass wall as the background for the Octagon House. Within the next two years, however, the AIA voted to renovate the Octagon House, purchase

the adjacent Lemon Building and redesign the proposed headquarters structure for 130,000 feet of floor space in contrast to the 80,000 called for in the competition.

Mitchell/Giurgola Associates prepared a new design (fig. 2) embodying the change in size. It differed in other ways from the competition winning design. The concave glass facade was gone and in its place were two vertically-walled floors at the base and five additional floors projecting forward over the garden in a series of reverse steps. At the rear of the building these five floors were enclosed by a slanted skylight.

A number of architects who reviewed the design feared that its cost would exceed the $30 per square foot that had been budgeted for the building. They received support from an unexpected quarter, on different grounds, when the Fine Arts Commission declared the design "out of keeping with the feeling of the Octagon" and rejected it. William Walton, Gordon Bunshaft and the

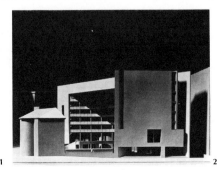

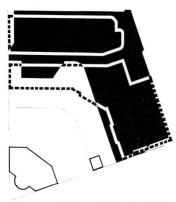

5 The former administration building and the Lemon building

By building to the maximum allowable building height of 90 feet (and thus blocking out adjoining buildings) a continuous backdrop for the Octagon was created.

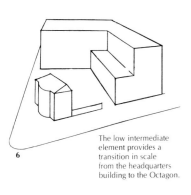

6 The low intermediate element provides a transition in scale from the headquarters building to the Octagon.

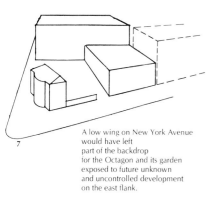

7 A low wing on New York Avenue would have left part of the backdrop for the Octagon and its garden exposed to future unknown and uncontrolled development on the east flank.

To create a successful scale relationship between the Octagon and the new headquarters building, it was necessary to maximize the distance between them. Further, this maximum distance increases the availability of southern light for the garden.

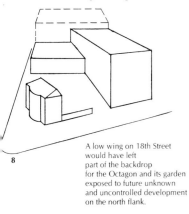

8 A low wing on 18th Street would have left part of the backdrop for the Octagon and its garden exposed to future unknown and uncontrolled development on the north flank.

other Commission members stated that the proposed design overwhelmed its elegant neighbor and reiterated their belief that the new building should be a quiet backdrop for the Octagon House.

Robert L. Durham, FAIA, then president of the AIA, stated for the record that the Institute's "belief in the need for the Fine Arts Commission and comparable design review boards throughout the country" led it to defer to the Commission's rejection and try again. Mitchell/Giurgola Associates produced still another design (fig. 3). In this design the height of the building was reduced, the set back from the Octagon House was increased and the floors were stacked vertically in the conventional way. A controversial design feature was the "notch" at the intersection of the two wings.

Once more the design was formally submitted to the Fine Arts Commission and this time, still under the influence of Bunshaft, the Commission balked at the notch and again rejected the building. Mitchell/Giurgola Associates refused to further compromise their design by restudying the notch and in September 1968, they resigned. By then George Kassabaum, FAIA, was president of the Institute, and he reiterated the principle that design review boards were "the best known means of maintaining order in the face of all of the pressures leading to chaos."

The AIA then proceeded to reorder the chaos into which its headquarters program had now fallen by appointing then-board member Max O. Urbahn, FAIA, to chair a committee to figure out what to do next. In December 1968 Urbahn recommended that a committee of architects be organized to select an architect. The board appointed Rex W. Allen, FAIA, Edward Charles Bassett, AIA, Romaldo Giurgola, AIA, G. Harold W. Haag, FAIA, Morris Ketchum, Jr. FAIA, Willis N. Mills, FAIA, I. M. Pei, FAIA and Philip Will Jr., FAIA. Urbahn agreed to be chairman. This committee proceeded to interview architects and finally selected Norman C. Fletcher of The Architects Collaborative to design the building. The latter chose TAC senior associate Howard F. Elkus to work with him on the project. Under Urbahn's leadership a series of informal meetings were held between TAC and the Fine Arts Commission during the design process. The formal approval went without a hitch, the funds were voted and the mortgage arranged.

The curved facade eliminates the appearance of separate wings or a central corner, and stresses the continuity and flow of the building around the garden from one street to the other.

The terrace cutback on the seventh floor of the headquarters building reduces the apparent height from the garden facade to six stories.

The diagonal masses, elements and lines of force visually link the headquarters building to the Octagon.

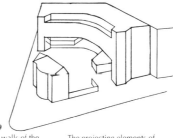

9

The old garden walls of the Octagon were rebuilt to link the Octagon with the new headquarters building and enclose the garden. The return of the wall at the New York Avenue entrance, and the old smokehouse at the 18th street entrance form zones of transition from these streets to the garden.

The projecting elements of the board room and executive suite recall the Octagon mass but are subordinate in height and size.

By partially recessing the street facade of the headquarters building, the block long mass of adjoining facades is interrupted and the building in its special setting is thus distinguished from its neighbors. The stair towers have been designed to relate to the geometry and massing of the Octagon while at the same time turning the corner.

The recess at the third story lightens the apparent mass of the office floors thus ameliorating and rendering more sympathetic the scale relationships between the headquarters building and the Octagon.

10

TAC's approach to the design of the building

Architects Fletcher and Elkus first made a feasibility study and plan for the redevelopment of the entire block (fig. 4). At the time a new Federal Deposit Insurance Company Building had been constructed at the end of the block opposite the Octagon House, but the area in between was occupied by a parking lot, an old hospital, townhouses and an office building. This TAC preliminary plan provided a central plaza between the proposed AIA building and the FDIC. The plaza would have had open arcades and several entrances from the adjoining streets. It was hoped that this provision of open space would have led to a

rezoning of building heights and densities to make the plaza economically feasible to prospective developers. The new headquarters building was to have opened directly on to the plaza, although the main entrance was, as now, on the garden side facing the Octagon.

As it turned out, the AIA was unable to achieve joint block planning. The developer of the hospital site replaced that building with one that extended to the AIA property line and deep into the center of the block, and the owners of the property on 18th street also maximized the use of their site. TAC, accordingly, eliminated the plans for an entrance and plaza at the rear of the building toward the center of the block.

The design
as built

The form of the new headquarters building (figs. 5, 6, 7, 8, 9) derived mainly from the requirement that as much space as possible be given to the Octagon House and its garden, while minimizing the scale of the new building. To this end the building utilizes considerably less square footage than the amount permitted by the local zoning. The principal access to the headquarters is through the plaza which is open to the sun and quite pleasant to walk through.

By extending continuous glass walls up to the third floor TAC has given the building the appearance of having been hollowed out, and thus it seems to draw back from the Octagon House. Elements which are smaller in scale than the Octagon House have been emphasized for contrast and balance. The conference room projects forward and its concrete walls contrast effectively with the glass facade (fig. 10). This element helps define the main entrance and shelters arriving visitors. The executive wing has been separately articulated as a scale transition.

The building is 90 feet high which is the maximum permitted in Washington, D.C. It was essential that the building be designed to this height in order to screen the neighboring buildings constructed on the AIA property line, especially as it became certain that these would be built to the maximum height. The top floor of the headquarters building is set back so that from all vantage points close to the building there appear to be six, rather than seven floors—another effective scale reducing device.

TAC's efforts to create as simple a backdrop for the Octagon House as possible prompted them to unite the north and east wings in a strong continuous curve that frames the garden. The interior organization of the building derives from this curve and the distinctive geometry of the site (fig. 11). The sweep of the building and the vectors of the site are combined in angled spaces, closer to the angles of a hexagon than those of a rectangle. These echo the angles of the Octagon House which is actually six-sided. Norman Fletcher likes to cite Frank Lloyd Wright's Hanna House in California as proof that such spaces flow more easily than 90 degree spaces. A triangulated ceiling system designed within this geometry which was an integrated structural, mechanical, electrical and com-

munications sandwich (August 1970, page 46) was abandoned because of cost and replaced by a conventional acoustical grid ceiling which is suspended from a single coffered slab.

The two ends of the building have been designed as simple shafts which incorporate the necessary stair towers. Their uninterrupted surfaces terminate the long sweep of the windows within the curve of the headquarters building (fig. 12). These towers also terminate the vistas down New York Avenue (fig. 13) and 18th Street, forming a two-sided frame for the Octagon House.

The original brick walls of the Octagon House and garden have been extended and refurbished. The old smokehouse, moved for a time during the construction, has been replaced in its original location. The original wooden gates of the property have also been restored. The brick sidewalks around the site have been relaid and repaired and the brick garden walks have been extended onto the larger terrace. This brick paving extends from the terrace into the ground floor exhibition area, thus integrating the old spaces and materials with the new.

TAC believes the other materials in the new building to be in sympathy with the Octagon House. The gray precast concrete relates well to the dark brick of the historic structure. Most importantly, the clear glass of the first two floors enables people outside to see the activity and the displays within.

The spatial organization within the building is as follows: two large underground floors house the garage, such services as printing and accounting, and mechanical equipment; the first three floors above ground are for AIA use, including the public exhibition space; and the top four floors are for tenants.

A new environment
for the AIA

Of most concern to TAC was the concept of the new AIA headquarters as a place where architects from all parts of the country will feel at home and like to return to. So far, members who have visited the new building are reacting positively. Norman Fletcher has noted with some pride that "the people of Washington cross the plaza on their walks. Already they enjoy the Octagon House and the garden. Soon they will see lively exhibits related to the arts, architecture and urban planning dis-

played in the exhibition hall and the adjoining plaza. We hope to have been successful in our attempt to design a building which provides for the daily needs of the profession *and* gives something back to the city."

The bisector of the intersecting perpendiculars to the angled streets shapes the basic geometry of the design solution

11

12

13

1033 MASSACHUSETTS AVENUE BUILDING, Cambridge, Massachusetts. Architect: *Hugh Stubbins and Associates—Hugh Stubbins, designer; Norman I. Paterson, project director.* Structural engineers: *LeMessurier Associates;* mechanical and electrical engineers: *Francis Associates;* contractor: *George B. H. Macomber Company.*

Though Massachusetts Avenue is the main corridor between Harvard University and Massachusetts Institute of Technology, it has remained an anonymous area, neither part of the academic communities nor a community in its own right. The office building above and on the following two pages (in part occupied and owned by its architect, Hugh Stubbins and Associates) is a new focal point for this street, enhancing it commercially while at the same time maintaining the scale and intimacy of Cambridge as a whole. The six-floor facade reflects the line of older buildings along the street and required parking is in the rear, off the street. The principal exterior material is concrete on both the poured-in-place columns and precast spandrel facings, all painted a light brown. The brown color is appropriate to the existing neighborhood, as exposed concrete might not be; paint eliminates water staining and the need for expensive formwork craftsmanship. The simplicity and cohesiveness of the facade is continued with the windows, which are straightforward spans of glass between the concrete. The facade as a whole gives a needed sense of closure to a fragmented but important street.

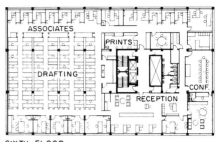

SIXTH FLOOR

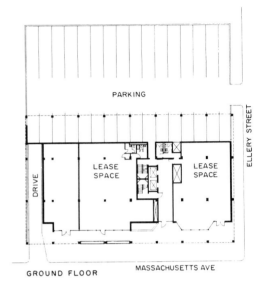

GROUND FLOOR

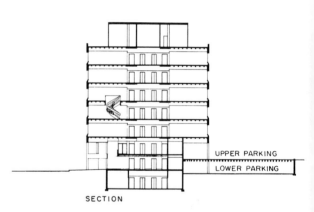

SECTION

Jonathan Green photos

At ground level the office building is undercut to widen the sidewalk; there are lively planting areas, a row of trees, and a giant "1033" painted on the brick front. The offices of Hugh Stubbins and Associates occupy the sixth and part of the fifth floors. The sixth floor (right, above) contains the main reception area, associates' offices, the library, conference rooms, print room, and drafting areas. Associates' offices ring the drafting area, separated from it by glass partitions, so that the open plan provides views of the Boston-Cambridge skyline for everyone. There are two levels of parking in the rear, approached from either Massachusetts Avenue or an adjacent side street. LeMessurier Associates, Inc., a Cambridge structural engineering firm, occupies the third and fourth floors, with a private stairway connecting them (see section, above). LeMessurier was the structural engineer for the building itself and has a financial interest in it with Stubbins.

A standard partitioning system was used throughout the building, on a 2-foot by 4-foot module. The partitions do not always meet the exterior wall at a column or mullion; a typical window is 6 feet high by 18 feet wide, with only one mullion within. Where a partition meets this glass surface, they are simply connected by a neoprene gasket, which is not disturbing from the outside. Stubbins' office designed all its own furniture, including drafting tables and low dividers. The office at left shows a particularly handsome birch desk; a full circle with about one-fourth of it sliced off to form a flat face for the chair.

NOXELL OFFICE BUILDING, Cockeysville, Maryland. Architects: *Skidmore, Owings and Merrill—partner-in-charge: William S. Brown; partner-in-charge of design: Gordon Bunshaft; project designer: Roger Radford; project manager: Frederick C. Gans; structural engineers: Weiskopf and Pickworth; mechanical engineers: Jaros, Baum and Bolles.*

Problems usually associated with the construction of an industrial complex—occasioned here by the consolidation of the Noxell Corporation's office, laboratory, production and storage facilities—were compounded by a desire to preserve the site, which previously had been a nursery, and to build on a human scale. The solution, calling for only two buildings with future expansion possibilities, makes outstanding use of cleanly articulated materials and forms.

The low-lying office-laboratory building was recessed into a sloping site (see section at right), so that only a one-story facade is exposed to the approach. An inner courtyard allows light to enter the otherwise windowless lower level. The storage-production plant is set low behind the office structure.

The structure permits a column-free space 115 by 300 feet. Open-web steel girders span between the white-painted exterior girders, which in turn are supported by eight reinforced concrete columns. Mechanical services are contained within the open-web girders. Gray, heat-absorbing-glass curtain walls are set back under the roof to form a sheltered arcade around the building. Administrative offices are on the upper level, while the lower level contains laboratory and storage areas. As can be seen in the plan at right, the lower level extends beyond the upper one; the extension contains an entrance for trucks to unload directly into the storage room. This entrance can be seen in the distant retaining wall in the photograph, lower right, taken from alongside the warehouse.

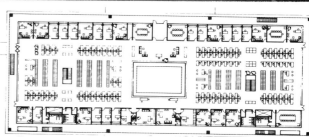

UPPER LEVEL

LOWER LEVEL

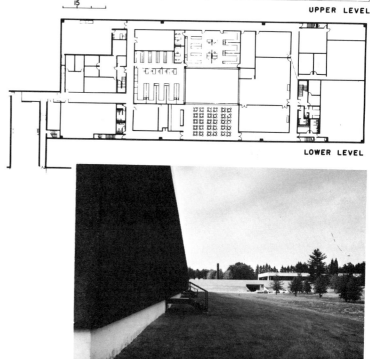

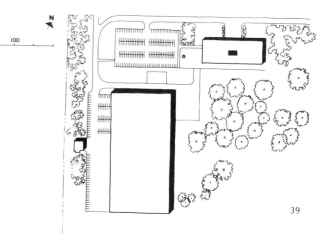

N

100

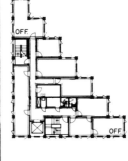

PACIFIC LUMBER COMPANY, San Francisco, California. Architects: *Ernest J. Kump Associates;* structural engineer: *Gilbert, Forsberg, Diekmann, Schmidt;* mechanical engineer: *Yanow and Bauer;* electrical engineer: *Sierra Electric Co.;* general contractor: *Plant Bros. Corp.;* landscape architect: *Royston, Hanamoto, Mayes & Beck.*

Meticulous detailing and controlled exuberance in uses of the client's wood products establish this corporate headquarters for Pacific Lumber Company as a dignified showcase that lives well with its colorful neighborhood—the site is a small, sloping triangular block in a somewhat Bohemian area near the San Francisco financial district. Since the building is wholly occupied by management staff in offices for one or two people, the limited spans of wood framing were suitable to the program. Rectangular bays expressed by engaged concrete columns with a sandblasted finish are arranged stepwise on the triangular site. Redwood detailing and exposed glue-laminated beams with a natural finish underscore the structural and decorative character of wood.

Interiors are carefully crafted in wood, including ceilings which are unusually detailed to demonstrate the variety of spatial enrichment the material offers.

Robert Brandeis photos

DELUCA CONSTRUCTION COMPANY, Stamford, Connecticut. Architects: *Sherwood, Mills, and Smith;* structural engineers: *Fromme and Vosganian;* mechanical engineers: *Smith and Hess.*

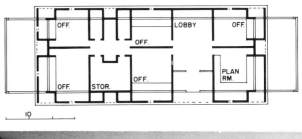

To overcome and hopefully upgrade a rundown residential-commercial neighborhood, architects A. Raymond von Brock and Robert Brady of Sherwood, Mills and Smith designed this low, simple rectangular building surrounded by a white stucco envelope hung over the enclosed area in such a way as to permit daylight to enter from below—reflected from a white gravel bed surrounding the building. Rhythmic penetrations of this curtain permit a sense of contact with the exterior without the intrusion of the unattractive neighborhood. All windows of the interior building are screened by the envelope but retain contact with the openings so that the interior is responsive to changes in outside light intensity. The interior building has a brick wall to sill height topped by a glass curtain wall to ceiling height.

A plaster relief composed of the letters in "Deluca" is opposite the entry, on the inside of the outer wall. Seen through the glass wall backing the reception room, it emphasizes the unusual lighting.

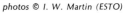

photos © I. W. Martin (ESTO)

PLASTER MURAL

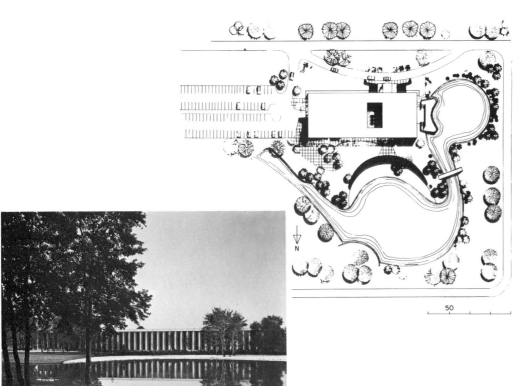

EXECUTIVE OFFICES, KLOPMAN MILLS, Rockleigh, New Jersey. Architects: *Schofield & Colgan;* structural engineers: *Fromme & Vosganian;* electrical engineers: *George London Associates;* mechanical engineers: *Frank A. McBride Company;* landscape architect: *Vincent C. Cerasi;* general contractor: *Fred J. Brotherton.*

The program for this two-story building, on a 15-acre suburban site, involved consolidation of several New York City office locations into a single home office and operations building. The corporate identity sought in the handling of cast stone columns and fascia set in park-like surroundings reflects the function of company headquarters and showrooms used for presentations to large buyers. A reflecting lake, man-made from swamp, partially surrounds the building.

The structure is steel frame with exterior walls of glazed buff brick veneer on concrete block. Bronze anodized aluminum window frames and glass spandrels form two-story panels between cast stone columns. Interior doors are teak veneer and executive offices are finished with teak, cherry, oak or butternut panelling. Floors are carpeted throughout.

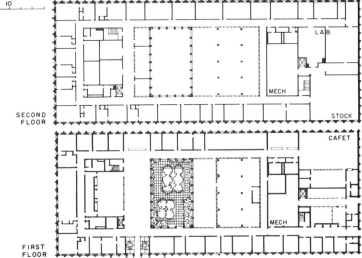

Internal functions include executive and clerical operations, a computer center, laboratories and showrooms. These are arranged in a two-level rectangle with an off-center landscaped court (shown at right). The entrance lobby creates a cross access along one side of this court and divides executive functions from middle management and clerical functions at the longer end of the rectangle.

A service entrance, cafeteria and laboratories are at the end of the building (far right in plan). The cafeteria and its exterior terrace overlook the lake. Similarly, an executive dining room on the first floor overlooks another portion of the lake.

SECOND FLOOR

LAB.

MECH.

STOCK

CAFET.

FIRST FLOOR

MECH.

G. M. WALLACE BUILDING, Denver, Colorado. Architects: *Moore & Bush;* structural engineer: *Edward R. Bierbach;* mechanical engineer: *Francis E. Stark;* electrical engineers: *Swanson Rink & Associates;* general contractor: *Brown-Schrepferman & Co.*

Adroit handling of low-cost materials (brick, concrete, glass and anodized aluminum) brings this two-level leaseback office building well within the competitive framework of its planned technological community near Denver. Chief tenant is a growing computer company, and core spaces of main (upper) level are accordingly adapted to computer, library and classroom spaces with peripheral offices. The first-floor level is partially below grade on three sides, preserving horizontal unity with nearby low buildings, and permitting pedestrian access at both levels.

Rush I. McCoy photos

Structure is poured-in-place concrete with exposed-aggregate concrete spandrels extended 4½ feet in sunshade hoods matching overhang of the concrete fascia. Mechanical facilities are in a low-profile penthouse and include absorption refrigeration for air conditioning.

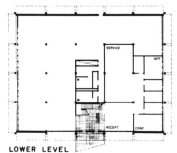

LOWER LEVEL

UPPER LEVEL

Joseph W. Molitor photos

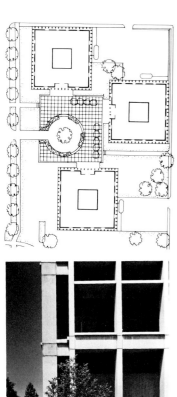

ADMINISTRATION BUILDING, Nutley, New Jersey. Owner: Hoffman-LaRoche. Architects: *Lundquist & Stonehill—Oliver Lundquist, partner, John Jay Stonehill, partner, Bryant Conant, project associate;* structural engineer: *Goldreich, Page & Thropp;* mechanical engineer: *Abrams & Moses;* electrical engineer: *Gustave P. Weiser;* acoustical consultant: *Ranger Farrell;* furnishing consultant to owner: *Joseph Whited;* mechanical contractor: *F. W. McBride;* electrical contractor: *Eastern States Electrical Contractors;* general contractor: *W. J. Barney Company.*

The new Hoffmann-La Roche headquarters building, designed by architects Lundquist & Stonehill, is a response to the client's need for a building that would have great flexibility, provide amenities for all levels of employees, and which could be designed and built quickly and reasonably. The building is the first of three to be located around a central plaza. The solution meets the client's needs with great skill and sophistication, and is a very effective example of a common building type too often handled without such meticulous attention to detailing.

Joseph W. Molitor

Robert Galbraith

The structure of the building is strongly expressed by the 5-foot set-back of the bronze-tinted glass wall. Columns, spandrels and sunshades are poured-in-place, reinforced smooth-finish concrete, contrasting with the vertical board finish of the ground-level walls and the exposed stair tower. The spandrels form a walkway around the building. The concrete columns are set every 7½ feet reflecting the interior module of 2½ feet. The sunshades provide good protection, with the west wall being in total shade until 4 o'clock and the south wall receiving less than 40 per cent of sun at 2 p.m. on October 21.

The stair tower was placed on the exterior not just for esthetic reasons, but for many functional reasons. Under local building code regulations, the second means of emergency exit also needs an adjoining air tower of 10 by 20 feet. If the second stair and its air tower were placed within the core, it would have disturbed the very low core/floor ratio of one to nine, as well as the efficiency of the core as a circulation point. The bold interior of the stair tower is shown in the construction photograph at left.

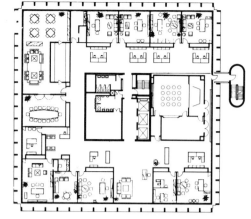

EXECUTIVE FLOOR

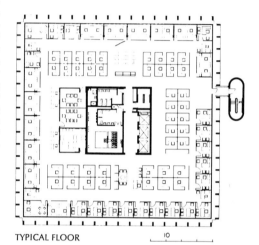

TYPICAL FLOOR

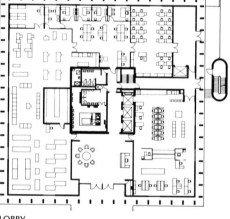

LOBBY

The painstakingly detailed design of this office building grew out of the client's need for complete flexibility. This need was interpreted by the architects and engineers by integrating the mechanical and electrical systems within the structural system. And flexibility in mechanical and electrical services has been achieved by development of a plug-in combination light and air supply or exhaust box which can be placed at random within a coffered ceiling, permitting concentration of light and air wherever it is needed. The coffered ceiling also serves as the anchor for a unique, custom-made clip-in partition system (see page 50). The result is a facility that can be easily adapted to the changing needs of the client.

Commensurate with the building's great flexibility is its provision of human amenities, as reflected in choice of materials and in meeting esthetic as well as functional requirements. The eight-story, square-plan building seems very warm in feeling for an all-concrete structure. The warm beige exterior concrete in two finishes—smooth by use of plastic-coated plywood forms for the columns and sunshades, and a rough, vertical board finish on the walls at ground level and on the exterior stair tower—relates in color to existing buildings on the site. The warmth of the exterior is enhanced by the use of bronze-tinted glass.

The architects took a more-than-functional approach to development of

the interior areas, with special consideration to choice of materials. The core-to-floor ratio is very low—one to nine—and this contributes to a sense of openness. This feeling is enhanced by ready proximity of any work place to the sheer glass wall behind the structural facade. The 10-foot clear ceiling height also contributes, with height added by the coffers.

Interior materials are simple and muted, being given added warmth by the use of incandescent light within the coffer-box system. The coffers cut off the light from 150-watt bulbs at an angle of 45 degrees. Interior finishes include exposed vertical board form concrete finish on the core, the oak wood, the matte black plastic accent and glass of the par-

Robert Galbraith

Robert Galbraith

The interiors are spacious, comfortable, and carefully detailed. The executive office floor, above, has special features, but within the basic system. Special plaster partitions with white sand paint finish contrast with the rough concrete finish of the core wall. Photo of a typical office floor, right, shows the column-free space, the glass wall set within the structural framework, and one arrangement of the flexible air/light plug-in ceiling units. Below is the waiting area in lobby.

Joseph W. Molitor

Robert Galbraith

The compact core occupies only 1,600 square feet (40 by 40 feet) of the usable 10,500 square feet per floor. With its 1-foot-thick concrete walls, it serves as a shear wall to provide lateral bracing for the structure. The thick walls also serve as a shield from the noise of the mechanical equipment located on each floor. The sub-lobby contains all required service components. The initial population of the building is 520, with an increase to 680 projected by 1975. Core facilities and elevators are adequate to serve 1,000 workers. The core was designed with two penetrations, a major and a minor one, for efficiency of movement within the building. The ¾-inch rough board vertical texture with tie holes exposed on the surface of the core walls, serves as a textural foil to other interior materials. The east elevation of the stair lobby, below, shows handling of phone, mail chute, emergency equipment and water fountain.

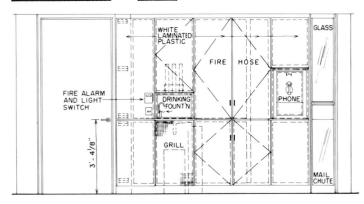

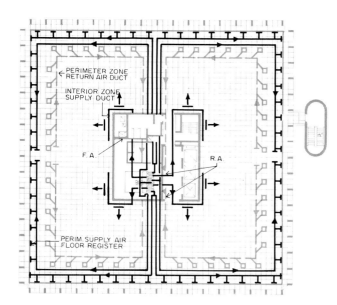

The air distribution diagram, above, shows the horizontal arrangement of supply and exhaust sources within the plenum created by the raised floor. Each floor operates independently, with great flexibility of arrangement possible. Below is a possible lighting arrangement with lighted coffers creating bright pools (approximately 90 footcandles) over work areas, with lower level illumination for circulation areas.

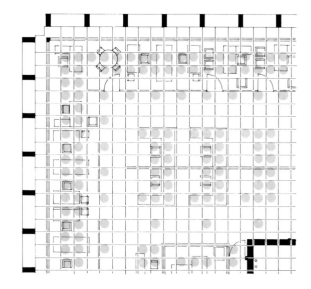

tition system, and carpeting throughout.

Structurally, the building has a 40- by 40-foot core with 1-foot thick shear walls that give lateral bracing to the structure. The exterior wall, set 5 feet out from a floor-to-ceiling glass wall, is a grid of 10- by 30-inch columns interconnected by sunshades and spandrels. The columns are set every 7½ feet to reinforce the interior planning module of 2½ feet. The spandrels form a walk around each floor, preventing any sense of acrophobia from the glass walls and allowing easy maintenance. Between core and exterior are 40-foot clear spans of waffle-slab concrete, creating the coffered ceiling.

The mechanical and electrical systems operate independently on each floor, permitting separate floors to be open in off hours and infinite flexibility on each floor. These systems are supplied and controlled from mechanical and electrical equipment shielded from noise within the thick core walls.

For interior areas there are metal air/light boxes which can be plugged into any coffer, serving as supply units for the interior and supply or exhaust on the perimeters. Each floor is raised above the coffered ceiling, forming an air plenum for electrical and communications wiring and ducts. Floor air outlets, set every 7½ feet between the structural bays, provide conditioned air for perimeter zones.

Speed of construction and budget were also factors in planning the building.

The building contains a total of 150,000 square feet and cost $4.8 million, making the cost per square foot $32 including lighting and basic air-distribution system, but not including the following: special air-conditioning requirements and tenant work on the executive floor, special installations in the computer area, full television studio in the basement, and underground energy center. The project was completed from design concept to finish in 26 months. Contributing to the fast construction were the hiring of a contractor on a cost-plus basis, separation of mechanical and electrical components from the structural system, and use of rapid construction systems such as the partitions and light/air boxes.

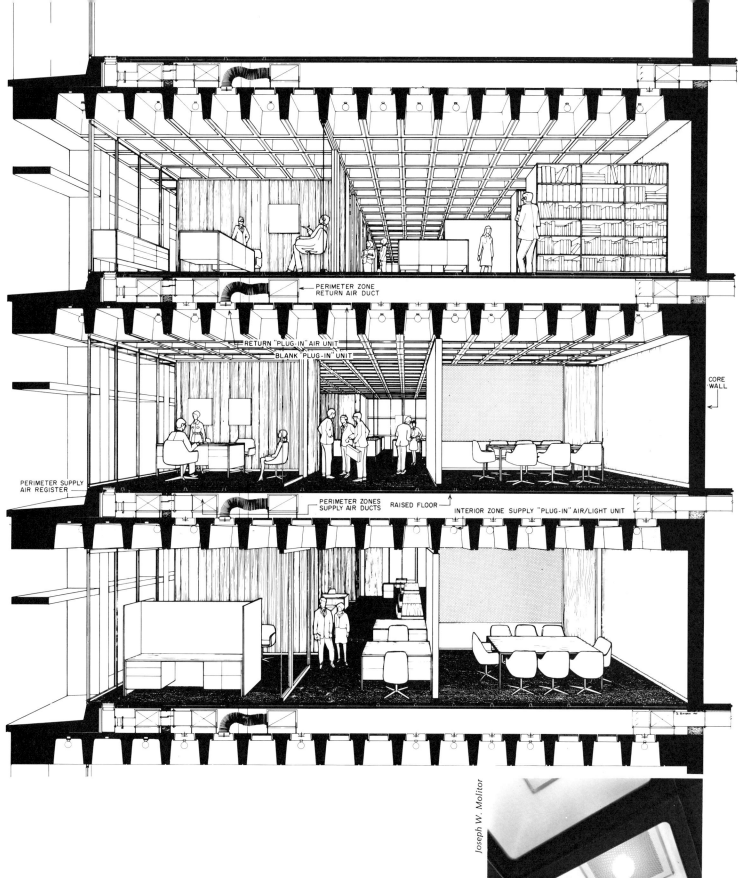

PERIMETER ZONE
RETURN AIR DUCT

RETURN "PLUG-IN" AIR UNIT
BLANK "PLUG-IN" UNIT

CORE
WALL

PERIMETER SUPPLY
AIR REGISTER

PERIMETER ZONES
SUPPLY AIR DUCTS   RAISED FLOOR

INTERIOR ZONE SUPPLY "PLUG-IN" AIR/LIGHT UNIT

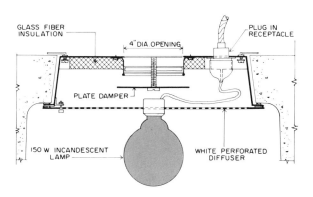

GLASS FIBER
INSULATION

4" DIA. OPENING

PLUG IN
RECEPTACLE

PLATE DAMPER

150 W INCANDESCENT
LAMP

WHITE PERFORATED
DIFFUSER

The air/light plug-in units are the
key to flexibility in lighting and
mechanical systems. The lighting
fixtures are in most areas incandescent, with a finely perforated plate
to diffuse the air. The plate hinges
to a metal air box with its simple
adjustable supply valve, and can be
inserted in every coffer. The 18-
inch-deep coffers provide a 45-
degree cut-off for the 150-watt
bulbs. Incandescent lighting was
chosen because of its warm color.

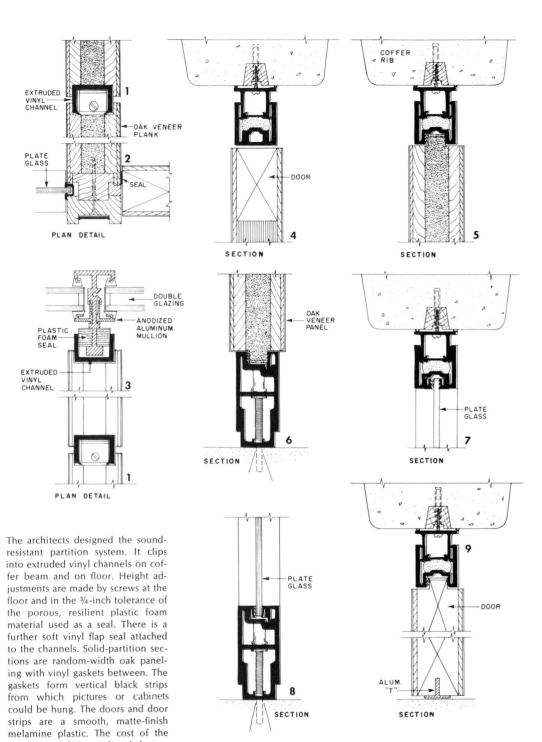

EXTRUDED VINYL CHANNEL

OAK VENEER PLANK

PLATE GLASS

SEAL

1

2

PLAN DETAIL

DOUBLE GLAZING

ANODIZED ALUMINUM MULLION

PLASTIC FOAM SEAL

EXTRUDED VINYL CHANNEL

3

1

PLAN DETAIL

COFFER RIB

DOOR

4

SECTION

5

SECTION

OAK VENEER PANEL

6

SECTION

PLATE GLASS

7

SECTION

PLATE GLASS

8

SECTION

9

DOOR

ALUM. "T"

SECTION

Joseph W. Molitor

The architects designed the sound-resistant partition system. It clips into extruded vinyl channels on coffer beam and on floor. Height adjustments are made by screws at the floor and in the ¾-inch tolerance of the porous, resilient plastic foam material used as a seal. There is a further soft vinyl flap seal attached to the channels. Solid-partition sections are random-width oak paneling with vinyl gaskets between. The gaskets form vertical black strips from which pictures or cabinets could be hung. The doors and door strips are a smooth, matte-finish melamine plastic. The cost of the system was $50 per lineal foot.

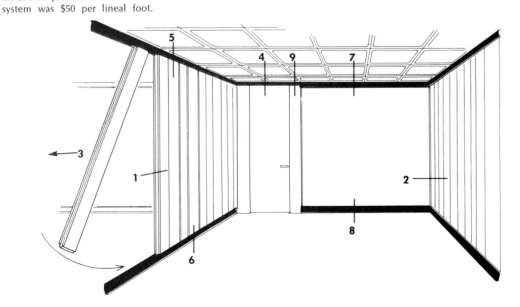

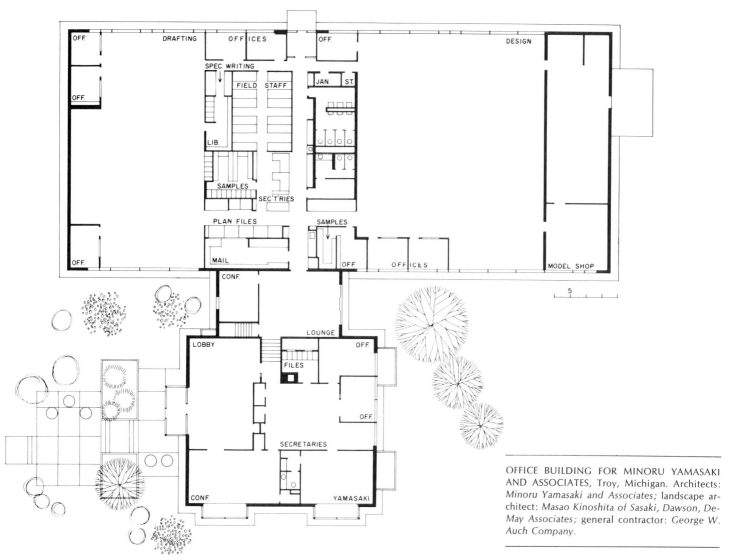

OFF.   DRAFTING   OFFICES   OFF.   DESIGN

SPEC. WRITING

FIELD   STAFF   JAN.   ST.

OFF.

LIB.

SAMPLES

SEC'T'RIES

PLAN FILES   SAMPLES

MAIL   OFF.   OFFICES   MODEL SHOP

OFF.

CONF.

5

LOUNGE

LOBBY   OFF.

FILES

OFF.

SECRETARIES

CONF.   YAMASAKI

OFFICE BUILDING FOR MINORU YAMASAKI AND ASSOCIATES, Troy, Michigan. Architects: *Minoru Yamasaki and Associates;* landscape architect: *Masao Kinoshita of Sasaki, Dawson, De-May Associates;* general contractor: *George W. Auch Company.*

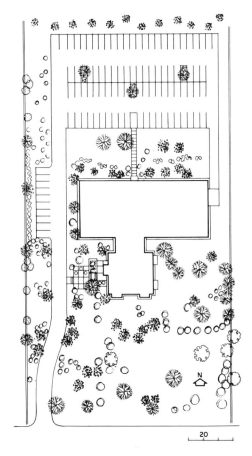

Yamasaki's own office building is unlike anything else he has done. Although it has the quality of expensive elegance which is typical of his best work, it is surprisingly simple. One looks in vain for traces of his luxuriant style—evocative plant forms in precast concrete with marble infill, or noble porticos with slender tapering columns ending in delicately pointed arches. In shaping his working quarters, the architect has chosen to abandon a more highly elaborated design vocabulary to display an unexpected mastery of the Miesian esthetic. Yama the client has convinced Yama the architect that this time "less is more."

"We wanted to be modest." said Yama. "We wished to avoid falling into the trap of building an office building as an advertisement. . . . We decided instead to carefully tailor a single-purpose building to our own special way of doing things. It is really for ourselves." And for themselves—seventy-five, plus or minus ten, including forty architects, twelve engineers and twelve model makers—Yama has created an exquisitely detailed and proportioned building, set within a five-acre site with beautiful trees, which he has landscaped with great care. "Our group," said Yama, "consists of highly trained and sensitive professional men who should have the kind of physical environment which can give dignity to their working lives. We felt that if we could build a quiet and tasteful building in a garden oasis, we could be happy and proud of the place in which we work."

The conference room (above), and Yama's office (below) are enhanced by deep bay windows shown in the exterior photo (opposite page). The entrance vestibule shown in the lobby photo and on the preceding pages is similar to the bay windows in detail. Sash and trim are stainless steel. Exterior walls are precast concrete.

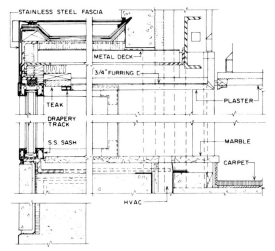

STAINLESS STEEL FASCIA

METAL DECK

3/4" FURRING

PLASTER

TEAK

DRAPERY TRACK

S.S. SASH

MARBLE

CARPET

HVAC

SECTION

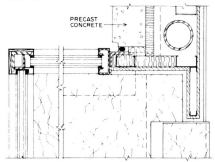

PRECAST CONCRETE

PLAN AT SILL

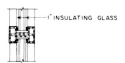

1" INSULATING GLASS

MULLION

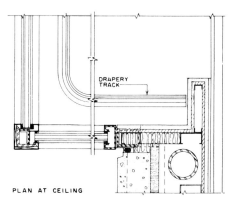

DRAPERY TRACK

PLAN AT CEILING

The administrative area is connected to the design and drafting wing by a linking element as can be seen in the photo (above left). The ground has been carefully sculptured to conceal the parking lot shown below. Drafting and design areas are spacious, allowing plenty of room for large scale models.

GENERAL OFFICE BUILDING, THE BOOTS PURE DRUG COMPANY LTD., Nottingham, England. Architects and engineers: *Skidmore, Owings & Merrill* (Chicago)—*William Hartmann, partner-in-charge; Bruce J. Graham, partner-in-charge of design; Philip W. Thrane, project manager; associate architects: York Rosenberg Mardall—Brian Henderson, partner-in-charge; John Vulliamy, project manager;* structural engineers: *Felix J. Samuely and Partners;* mechanical engineers: *Matthew Hall Mechanical Services Ltd.;* quantity surveyors: *Gleeds;* landscape architect: *Kenneth Booth;* general contractor: *Taylor Woodrow Construction.*

© *Ezra Stoller (ESTO) photos*

In keeping with the Boots Pure Drug Company's dual plan requirement for readily mutable space allowing maximum flexibility in the layout of individual departments, plus more conventional spaces for relatively static functions, office areas are disposed on two levels around a sunken central courtyard (above). Wholly open, column-free space is concentrated on the upper, first-floor level, while the below-grade main ·floor, which receives natural light from the interior court, houses fixed facilities and those requiring only limited possibilities for rearrangement.

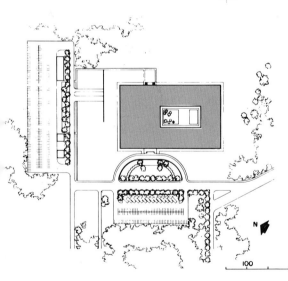

Though two-storied, the building reads from the outside as a low-slung, single-story mass. Soil from excavation was graded up around the concrete-walled main floor so that only the first floor emerges from the ground. Visually scaling down the 480- by 288-foot mass to compatibility with its meadowland setting, this solution also conforms to the practical plan requirements of the building, and the structure devised to meet them. The below-grade main floor, needing less flexibility, is reinforced concrete with relatively small (24-foot) column bays within the perimeter retaining wall, while the upper floor owes its 120,000 square feet of unimpeded space to steel columns and girders with 96-foot clear spans. Only at the main entrance are both floors open to the outside, allowing employees to enter and leave the building at the level where they work. Thus, most vertical traffic circulates on the exterior, and the need for vertical access within the building is kept to a minimum.

Rising some 2½ feet above grade, the visible upper portion of the main-floor retaining wall forms a recessed base for the open first-floor level, which is enclosed by a crisply detailed bronze-anodized aluminum window wall with spandrels that repeat the pale gray granite used for the entrance steps. The freestanding structural frame is of black-painted steel, with cruciform columns shaped for unambiguous definition at building corners, and proportioned (at 30 inches across) to support visually as well as actually the massive (6-foot, 3-inch) girders required to bridge the 96-foot bays.

The central courtyard functions on the most prosaic level as a light well—and, because of its 100- by 200-foot expanse, also reinforces the building's pervasively open quality, affording workers stationed in "interior" areas the same sense of space-extended enjoyed by their counterparts with views to the fine landscape outside. While fully reflecting the building's formidable size and almost equally formidable precision of finish, the court is yet an urbanely human space, livened by the play of natural elements —the water of the reflecting pool, the greenery of the planted area—and by the color and movement of people glimpsed behind its transparent enclosure.

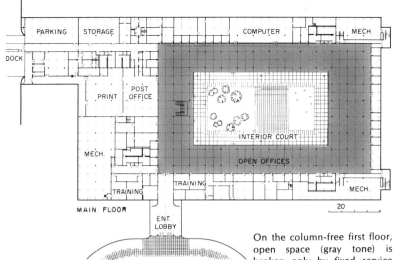

MAIN FLOOR

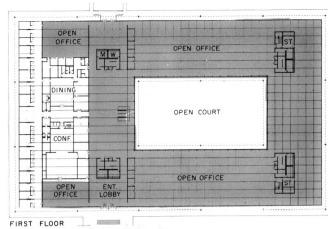

FIRST FLOOR

On the column-free first floor, open space (gray tone) is broken only by fixed service elements (stairs, toilets and cloakrooms). Executive offices, the only conventional offices in the building, lie along the north wall, separated from the rest of the floor by such support facilities as private dining and board rooms. Specialized functions (data processing, training, conference, printing, postal, and storage facilities, and mechanical space) that need little flexibility and no outside exposure are ranged around the perimeter of the below-grade main floor; office areas requiring more latitude in layout, as well as light and view, are concentrated in the open space around the central court.

Entrance to main floor lobby (above) introduces the restrained use of warmly neutral colors and textures, and the sense of uncluttered space, that distinguish the building's interiors—all designed by the architects. *Cafe au lait* carpeting and richly grained natural oak finishes are used throughout, with additional, still subtle, color lent by bronze-tinted-glass office partitions, which admit light while assuring a measure of acoustic privacy.

The 5-foot, 8-inch-high natural oak carrels which replace standard office cubicles in all open areas may be either three-sided or four-sided, depending on the occupants' need for privacy and/or wall space. Made up of interchangeable components, carrels, like unpartitioned work stations, may be dismantled and rearranged at will to meet changing departmental needs—but always within a discipline established by the architects in advance and in absentia.

Alternate placement of work stations within the open plan is gently but effectively controlled by the need to conform to the pre-set pattern dictated by an underfloor grid of power and telephone raceways. This feeds required services to desktop outlets through access panels built into pedestal units.

SCOTT, FORESMAN AND COMPANY
Glenview, Illinois. Architect: *The Perkins
& Will Partnership;* landscaping: *Grund-
strom Company, Inc.;* consultants: *Architectural Concrete Consultants, Inc.;* contractor: *A. L. Jackson Company.*

The potential of a 44-acre site
in a residential suburb was used
to develop a remarkable working
environment in this new corporate
headquarters for Scott, Foresman
and Company, a large publisher
of educational materials. The
architects and their interior design
subsidiary—ISD Incorporated—
were commissioned to program
and plan the buildings with the
interiors as direct extensions
of the architecture. Further,
great stress was made in the
program for the use of materials,
scale and landscaping that would
be compatible with both
rather special working needs
and the neighborhood. Thus,
although the company is a
sizable one—with most functions
inter-related—an analysis
proved the feasibility of
dividing functions into four
linked buildings in a campus-
like cluster around courtyards.

A

B

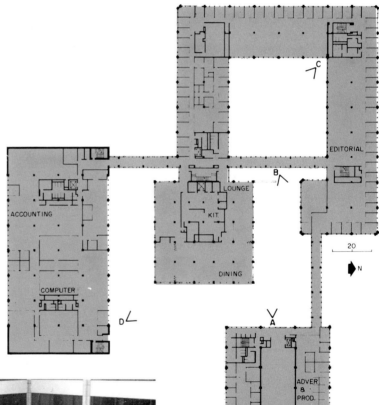

EDITORIAL

ACCOUNTING

LOUNGE

KIT.

DINING

COMPUTER

ADVER & PROD.

RECEPT.

20

N

C

In an almost idealized "bubble chart" fashion, publishing facilities in this complex are grouped into four buildings (executive functions, distribution and customer service, editorial, and central services and dining), all linked by glassed-in corridors or bridges at the appropriate levels. The areas between have been landscaped into very attractive and usable courts: view A (above left) is from the executive building, across a pool-centered mall to the editorial building; B is the same area, from the opposite direction, and shows the outdoor stairs leading to the lower-level editorial court shown in view C. A tree-studded court, D, separates the executive unit from the central building with dining facilities on ground level and library and meeting rooms on the upper level. Basic materials are brick and concrete.

D

CROWN CENTER OFFICE COMPLEX, Kansas City, Missouri. Owner: *Crown Center Redevelopment Corporation.* Architects: *Edward Larrabee Barnes, FAIA—associates: John M. Y. Lee, Edward Z. Jacobsen.* Associated architects: *Marshall & Brown—partner-in-charge: Jack E. Lakey.* Engineers: *Marshall & Brown* (structural); *Joseph R. Loring & Associates* (mechanical/electrical). Consultants: *Don Bliss Architectural Lighting Consultant* (lighting); *Peter G. Rolland & Associates* (landscape); *Harper & George, Inc.* (graphics). General contractor: *Eldridge Construction Company.*

As the initial gesture in Hallmark Cards Inc.'s long-range development plan for Crown Center, the design of the office complex was extremely important. These buildings had to make an impact on the gray area surrounding the Hallmark plant. They were to symbolize and pre-figure the quality of the architectural environment to come. It was essential that this office space please prospective tenants with its own intrinsic amenity, enticing them to sign leases and move in. All that Crown Center promises and has accomplished would never have begun had the office complex failed to attract tenants. Fortunately it has, due in large part to the quality of its architecture.

The buildings are each only seven stories high. The office workers, therefore, are physically close to the office plaza and its life. Although the structures are linked on alternate floors, each has its own entrance contributing to separateness and identity. The buildings step down the slope as do the terraced lawns they overlook. The quiet restraint of their architectural expression makes them an appropriate background for all the public activity which Hallmark hopes to generate in the plaza.

The plan configuration (right), provides flexible rentable square footage and office arrangements. The individual buildings range from 80,000 to 157,000 total square feet, with whole floors ranging from 8,600 to 28,000 square feet. Taken together, all five buildings comprise 626,300 square feet. Large 30-foot clear spans and five-foot modules contribute to the flexibility.

Underneath the offices is a six level 934,-000 square foot garage with 2,300 reserved spaces for tenants. Maximum security prevails in the garage and office spaces through the use of television monitoring, special lighting and a uniformed security force. The combined garages underneath the office complex and the hotel provide a total of 7,000 parking spaces.

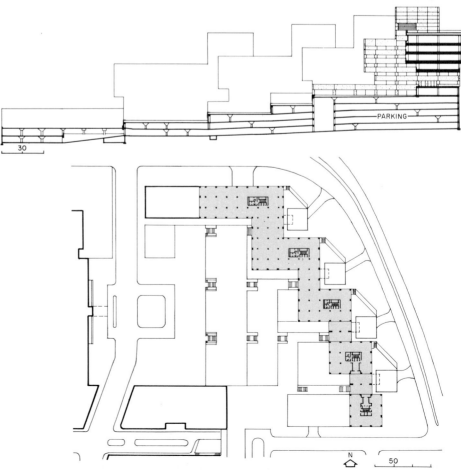

The fountain, designed by architect Barnes, is composed of 49 water jets, placed seven feet apart under special gratings. Water heights from each jet can be adjusted to any point between zero and 25 feet. This individual jet regulation permits the creation of such two-dimensional water patterns as a triangle, circle or square, as well as three-dimensional pyramids or cubes of water suspended within the whole. The 2,000 square foot fountain floor is paved with flat cobblestones and surrounded by a 23-foot apron of granite blocks. Below each water jet is a 300-watt colored light which automatically turns on at dusk, forming colored patterns within the flowing water. When the fountain is turned off, the cobblestoned floor and surrounding apron area become part of the larger plaza. An almost imperceptible incline allows for drainage and recycling back to the 8,000 gallon tank located in a nearby underground garage. The water flows at the rate of 3,500 gallons per minute.

The proportions of window to spandrel, and the modular organization of the precast panels have the elegance for which Barnes is famous. The proportions are equally handsome from within. The continuous bands of window glass range up to 750 linear feet per floor.

ONTARIO MEDICAL ASSOCIA-
TION OFFICE BUILDING, Toronto,
Canada. Architects: *A. J. Diamond
& Barton Myers—Ken Viljoen,*
project architect; cost control:
*Helyar, Vermeulen, Rae, & Mau-
chan;* structural engineers: *M. S.
Yolles & Assoc.;* mechanical engi-
neers: *G. Granek & Assoc.;* electri-
cal engineers: *J. Chisvin & Assoc.;*
general contractor: *Richard &
B. A. Ryan Limited.*

A quiet Toronto street in one of
the city's older residential sections
has a new office building on it,
housing the headquarters facilities
for the Ontario Medical Association, and the building may be a
little puzzling to any of the neighborhood people who have seen it
both inside and out. The street
facade is simple, almost conservative and haphazard in its flatness,
with its simple punched holes for
large windows that are in nearly
the same plane as the brick, and
with two large openings at either
end of the building that obviously
lead up from and down to a
parking garage below. Though
there are details around the
entrance that tell a trained eye
(or an architect) that the inten-
tions of the designers here were
serious, complex, and probably
meant as a challenge, still the
effect of the street facade is quite
unremarkable. But the effect of
the inside spaces, as in the photo
at left, is not. Walls rise through
three floors with clerestory lighting at the top, exterior light is
brought through two separated
planes of glass causing the darker
interior glass to reflect the image
of the lighter exterior walls, and
common electrical ducts are exposed on the wall surfaces along
with their outlet boxes and warm
and cold air piping. It is the combination of "averageness" on the
facade, the spectacular display of
spatial gymnastics inside, and the
use of usually concealed ducts as
decoration that would be surpris-
ing to any layman.

To the architects A. J. Diamond and Barton Myers, of course,
it is an expression of their con-
victions regarding architecture, and
what they believe should be made
important in their buildings. Both
architects worked in the office of
Louis Kahn, and they both ac-
knowledge the influence on them
of Robert Venturi's ideas. They
have not been interested in elaborated structure—in exposing the
bones of their buildings—but they
have been concerned with expressing the activities of people. They
say about the O.M.A. Building:
"Instead of expending funds and
energy on 'architecture' which in
truth often means structural exhi-
bitionism, or conspicuously expensive finishes, or excessive 'articula-

Karl Sliva

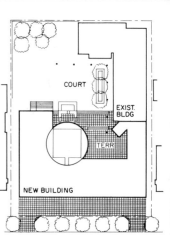

COURT

EXIST.
BLDG

TERR

NEW BUILDING

Ian Samson photos

tion' judgments made were in reference to the importance of activities, and user work requirements." The three principal activities within the O.M.A. are the administrative functions of the permanent staff, the executive function, which is carried out periodically (at least once every month) by meetings of the board of representatives, and the entertainment, dining and social functions of the association.

It is easy to see from the plans (page 75) which of these functions has been given symbolic emphasis over the others, and to understand why. The board meetings, at which decisions are made regarding the daily operations and ultimate public values of the Ontario medical profession, are the raison d'etre of the O.M.A. itself, and the board room has thus been made the center of attention of the whole design. It is circular where the rest of the spaces are rectilinear, and it is one of the largest spaces in plan, much larger than its programmed 40-person seating capacity might require. It exudes a kind of elegance (page 76) that the rest of the building has tried to avoid.

The other two activities interlock spatially throughout the rest of the building: the areas available for entertainment and public functions are on the ground floor, and executive or administrative functions occur on the upper two floors. The main lounge on the first floor (photograph at left) is near the entrance for large public dinners or receptions, the employees may use it during the working day and at lunch, and it is immediately available before board meetings. The major space of the administrative area is the secretarial pool on the second floor (photo, page 74). It rises through two floors, acknowledging its use by the largest daily concentrations of people, and the low-ceilinged one- and two-man offices surround the secretarial area on two floors. Finally, these activities are linked through three floors by the interior open space around the board room; the curved wall of the board room is visible from all floors and is the architectural event by which visual orientation is possible from any other place in the building.

The interior feeling of most of the O.M.A. Building is one of casualness. Except for the board room there is a kind of studied devaluation of hierarchies which is implied by the spatial interlocking of activities just described. But it is easy to notice Diamond's and Myers' other efforts to make the building unpretentious and to relax it: such information is supplied most clearly by the detail-

ing; the selection of fixtures and finishes, and the small parts of the building chosen for emphasis. The cold and warm air ducts of the mechanical system are directly exposed to view, and sometimes used as sculpture in space, as with the ductwork (below, left) leading from the entrance foyer to the conference room. The ducts are common spiral tubing of galvanized steel with the usual flexible elbows of aluminum, all with a white enamel finish baked on before installation. There are chromed splicing straps at each joint and chromed hangers. Their impact lies in their obvious commonness—even laymen know these things are usually hidden in basements or ceilings—and in their formal organization. The same judgments apply to the common tubing used as handrails, and to the lighting—ordinary flexible conduit and four-way outlet boxes have been exposed throughout the building in expressive, decorative ways (see photo, page 74).

The O.M.A. building's emphasis on the expression of human activities, and the architects' lack of commitment to any basic structural clarity certainly add up to a kind of devaluation of technological issues; the architecture doesn't much exhibit a concern for technical expression or even for rationalism, with its usual scientific emphasis. A kind of technical rationalism has always been one of the firmest foundations of modern architecture, and the attack on it here is refreshing to see. This building seems to say that of course technology is with us, but it need not be quite so revered: there are more important things to think about.

Even the exposure of mechanical and electrical parts says this; or more correctly, they especially say this. The electrical tubing, the outlet boxes, and the air ducts chosen are mass-produced in thousands of shapes and sizes; they are not specialized forms like LeCorbusier's "object-types," and they are utterly devalued artistically. In the construction industry, they are akin to consumer parts; purchased in quantity, nearly disposable. We have no reverence for these forms; they give us a light feeling of shock, of restraints removed, of casualness and wit.

The architects of this small office building have succeeded in expressing the human values and institutional organizational patterns which sponsored the building in the first place, as they intended to do. It is a successful building on that level, and at the same time it manages to impart new meaning to some of the inexpensive materials of our building industry.

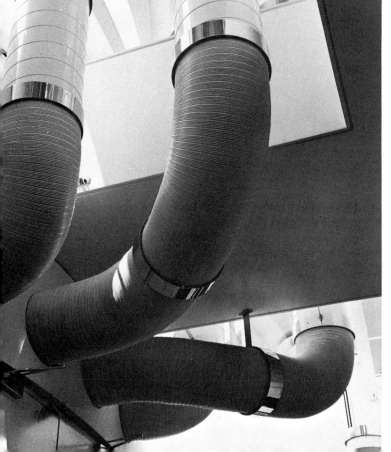

Ian Samson photos

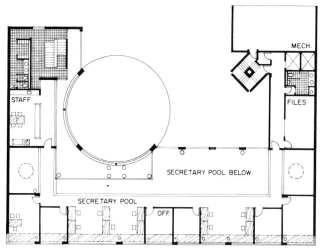

MEZZANINE

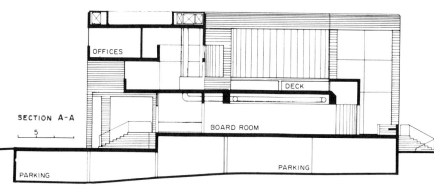

SECTION A-A

5

OFFICES

DECK

BOARD ROOM

PARKING

PARKING

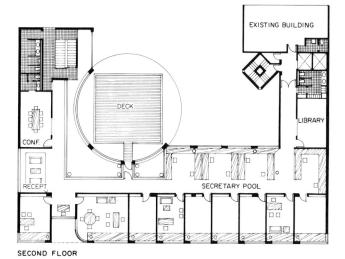

SECOND FLOOR

EXISTING BUILDING

CONF.

RECEPT.

SECRETARY POOL

LIBRARY

The new O.M.A. Building replaces an older residential structure on the same site that was previously used as the headquarters. The parts of the plans at left labeled "existing building" were a recent addition to that older residence that was allowed to remain. Together, the new O.M.A. headquarters and the existing building form two sides of a new court that will be the focus for any future expansions that may take place. The additions will be sited on the two remaining sides of the court, forming, eventually, an interior plaza. This focus toward the back of the building in the expansion plans and in the present bricked terrace, plus the existence of the large underground parking facilities (see section, above) keep the O.M.A. headquarters from encroaching into the street and neighborhood with its present and planned activities.

The main secretarial pool (photo, far left) faces out onto the rear court and is surrounded by two levels of offices. By exposing the mechanical ducts and eliminating hung ceilings, floor-to-floor heights were reduced to 8 ft-6 in. in most areas.

A

COURT

EXISTING BUILDING

COATS

BOARD

TERRACE

RECEPT.

ENTRANCE

LOUNGE

TEL

CONF.

KIT

RAMP DN

A

MAIN FLOOR

10

The board room of the O.M.A. Building (photo, above) is prominent from any point of view around the building and its roof has been employed as a deck for lounging; placing a square within a circle allows seating on the parapet, because any seat is usually a safe distance from the edge.

The standard spiral metal ducts in the building, like those in the photo at left, were cut to fit from shop drawings in a factory, rather than formed at the site. Each section of duct received an inexpensive white baked enamel finish which could not have been applied using site fabrication. The isometric (page 77) is the clearest representation of the new O.M.A. building, and indicates the architects' de-emphasis of exterior facades; the major significance lies in the spaces (both exterior and interior) and with the interior parts.

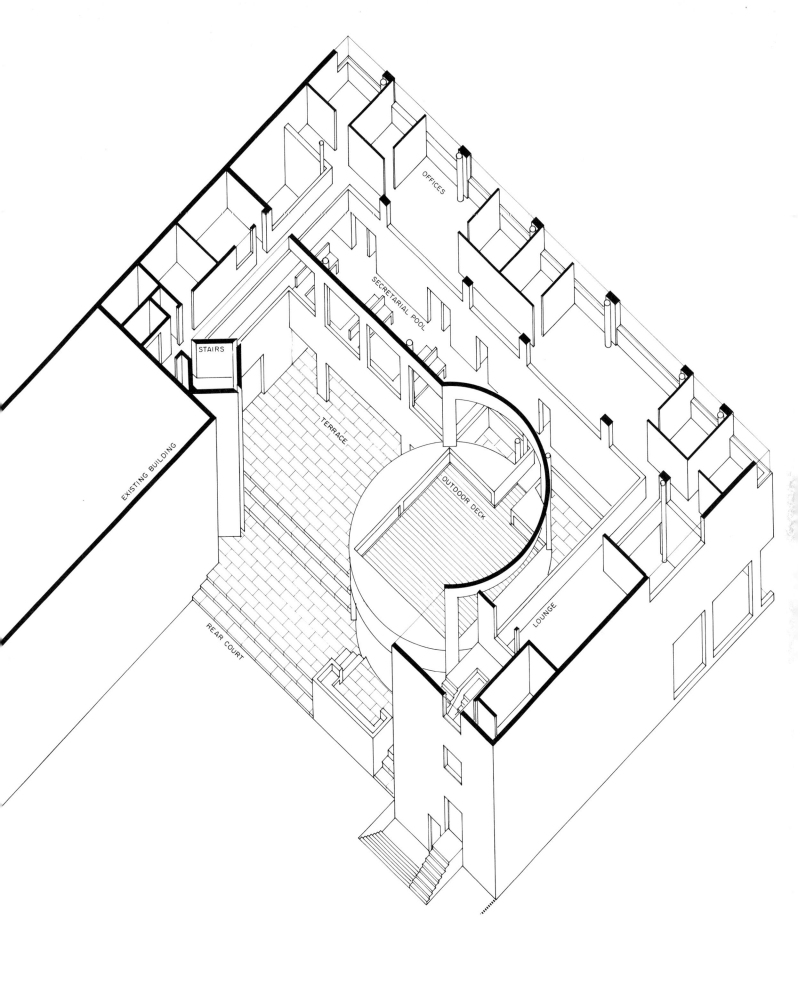

OFFICES

SECRETARIAL POOL

STAIRS

EXISTING BUILDING

TERRACE

OUTDOOR DECK

REAR COURT

LOUNGE

The principal stairway of the O.M.A. Building rises from the parking garage to the third floor. The open doorway of the photo above looks through to the second floor level, and the picture at left was taken below the first floor, looking straight up. The very simple but effective detailing of the building is especially evident here, along with the absence of expensive materials or finishes.

BURROUGHS-WELLCOME CO., Research Triangle Park, North Carolina. Architect: *Paul Rudolph;* engineers: *Lockwood-Greene Engineers, Inc.;* contractor: *Daniel Construction Co.*

Springing in inclined forms from the summit of a long ridge
in North Carolina's Research Triangle Park, the laboratory
and corporate headquarters of the Burroughs-Wellcome Co. is marked
by the sculptural invention that has long made Paul Rudolph's
work so arresting. It is also filled with the characteristic
complexities that make his work, in some quarters, controversial.

The client wanted a building that was shaped to his needs
but remained architecturally distinctive—a building that would
leave a forceful after-image in the minds of all who see it.
Rudolph wanted the building to be a man-made extension of the ridge.
He also wanted an opportunity to explore the variety of spatial
relationships that diagonal framing could produce.

Viewed from almost any vantage point, Burroughs-Wellcome is a large and complex structure. It encloses some 300,000 square feet of laboratory and administrative space distributed unevenly over five stories. In plan, the building forms a giant "S" with opposing arms that embrace a main entry court and a large service yard. Reception, cafeteria, library, auditorium and administrative offices flank the entry court. Laboratories, research offices and quarters for test animals surround the service yard.

The handsomely textured exteriors are finished in a limestone aggregate which is sprayed in place to a plastic binder. The same finish is used selectively inside.

Flexibility was a primary programmatic goal. Each major area in Rudolph's plan—laboratories, administration and support services—can be expanded by simple, linear addition. To prepare for this eventuality, the architect left the expansible ends of the building expressed in a somewhat random pattern of flattened hexagons (photos right). Any of the elements can be extended horizontally without disturbing the building's visual order. This device, combined with an elaborate articulation of parts, complicates the elevations considerably but gives the building an agreeable scale and plunges it squarely into the realm of dynamic architectural sculpture. The complications of the exterior assert themselves inside with no less force. The three-story lobby space (photo page 83) closes dramatically overhead in a turbulent and visually compelling spatial composition. The administrative offices are shaped at the exterior wall to receive skylights that admit daylight from an unseen

(text continued on page 82)

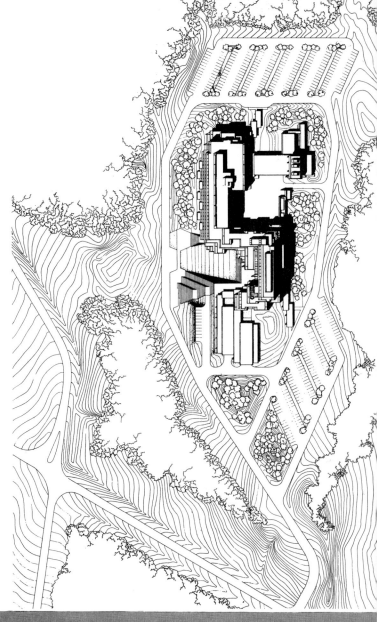

The site is 66 acres of rolling woodland approximately equidistant between Raleigh, Durham and Chapel Hill. Because Burroughs-Wellcome is research oriented, its ties to the three surrounding universities are immediate and vital. Much of the rolling woodland has been left intact and new planting around the building and in the parking areas will gradually heighten the site's natural qualities.

and unexpected source. The board room, over the cafeteria, opens out through a canted window wall to one of the fairest scenes in North Carolina: a timbered Piedmont plain with the spires of Chapel Hill in the distance.

The structure is an eccentrically loaded, trapezoidal steel frame with columns inclined at 22½ degrees (see section at right). To absorb the substantial bending moments, floor beams and columns are linked in the transverse direction by rigid moment connectors. Tie beams, below grade, take up the horizontal component of all gravity loads.

Throughout the building, the inclined columns seem to emerge, disappear and re-emerge freely. When they lie in the plane of a wall, they are simply integrated without fussy detail. When they stand independently, the space flows around them with only the merest hint of obstruction. Diagonal relationships are present everywhere and right-angled elements, when they appear, do so almost apologetically. The spaces are particularized and personal; as much the opposite of universal space as Rudolph could make them. A simple and consistent vocabulary of finishes gives the administrative areas an easy continuity and flow.

The Burroughs-Wellcome building is not for those who are disturbed by departures from the norm. The sharp-eyed visitor may find details that are not completely resolved. But if there is bravura here, it is more than balanced by solid accomplishment. The building is functional—probably no more and no less so than similar facilities of more routine design. What is best about Burroughs-Wellcome is the sense of exhilaration and spatial excitement it awakens. That it achieves so much of each is a tribute to both architect and owner.

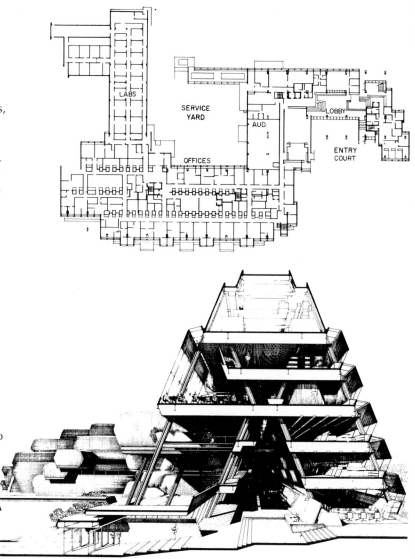

Diagonal lines of force make themselves felt throughout. The sloping shafts that line the corridors are used for storage and for housing the heavy mechanical service requirements of the laboratory and research spaces.

HIGH-RISE
OFFICE BUILDINGS

Each of the 16 high-rise office buildings which follow is noteworthy for one or a combination of reasons, but the most significant are so by virtue of their technology. One of the two most interesting is the Knights of Columbus building in New Haven, Connecticut (pages 95–102). Because a tall slender building was desired, the area of the typical floor had to be reduced. To this end, the elements which are usually placed in the core—stairs, toilets and mechanical shafts—were located in round concrete silos at each of the four corners. These towers serve as the basic structural supports of the building. Only the elevators are located in the core.

The second work of major technological interest is the Federal Reserve Bank of Minneapolis (pages 157–161). Here an office block has been designed to span 275 feet by means of two catenary members 60 feet apart and suspended from two great concrete towers.

The visionary idea of an office building as a collection of industrially manufactured capsules became a reality with the completion of the Nagakin Capsule Tower Building in Tokyo (pages 117–119). The prefabricated one-man capsules containing a bed, chair, closets, desk, tape deck, TV and bathroom are attached to steel frames supported by reinforced concrete rigid-framed towers.

Precast technology has been advanced by Brook Hollow Plaza in Dallas, Texas (pages 154–156). Except for the floors within the core, this high-rise is an assembly of precast parts including the columns, spandrels, floor planks and core walls.

Roger Sturtevant photos

BANK OF AMERICA WORLD HEADQUARTERS, San Francisco, California. Architects: *a joint venture of Wurster, Bernardi and Emmons and Skidmore, Owings & Merrill—Pietro Belluschi, consulting architect.* Landscape architects: *Lawrence Halprin and Associates;* structural engineer: *H. J. Brunnier and Associates;* mechanical and electrical engineers: *Skidmore, Owings & Merrill;* acoustical consultants: *Bolt Beranek and Newman;* lighting consultants: *Seymour Evans Associates;* graphics consultants: *Barbara Stauffacher Solomon,* audio-visual consultant: *Henry Jacobs;* plaza sculpture: *Masayuki Nagare;* fountain consultants: *Beamer/Wilkinson and Associates.* Contractors: *Dinwiddie-Fuller-Cahill,* a joint venture.

The new Bank of America tower in San Francisco—a joint venture of Wurster, Bernardi and Emmons, Skidmore, Owings & Merrill, and with Pietro Belluschi as consulting architect —is a delicately changing piece of sculpture to the pedestrian in the city. It is faceted, like finely cut crystal, into a thousand surfaces that change their patterns and color depending on the angle at which you see them; the facade can appear to be long, square tubing bundled together with the corners showing, or it is zig-zagging horizontal lines, or it is a checkerboard seen in perspective. It is a building that makes its transitions well, like San Francisco itself. The rhythm of constant corners along one facade prepares the eye for the real corner and the adjacent facade; one hardly knows where the 90-degree change in plane has been made. It has a top that ends assertively and in proportion to the whole; the building could not as successfully have been ten stories shorter or taller. As the eye moves to the ground a projected bay becomes an indented bay at the second floor, while the column faces remain in the same plane. The Bank of America tower is uniquely suited to a city where the bay window has been traditional since the 19th century. The tower has become, and will remain a key architectural monument in San Francisco.

Two decisions were made almost at once by the architects—1) the building should be dark in color, 2) it should not be an austere rectangular box—and the results of these decisions are the tower's most significant attributes. Its faceted, flowing walls provide a continuous rhythm of interior and exterior bays around the facade, as these photos indicate. The bay window is a strong element in San Francisco's cityscape, variously explained as a way of bringing in more light on dark foggy days and as a means of obtaining more floor space than a building lot provides. The windows greatly enliven vistas along hilly streets and preclude monotony with their undulating rhythms. The Bank of America's walls are thus a modern, abstracted, version of a regional tradition, and are easily recognizable by citizens as a link with the best parts of their past.

The views looking east along Pine Street (above) and west along Pine Street (right) indicate the

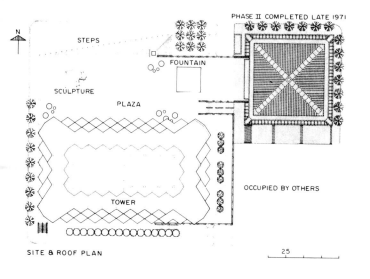

N

STEPS

SCULPTURE

FOUNTAIN

PLAZA

PHASE II COMPLETED LATE 1971

TOWER

OCCUPIED BY OTHERS

SITE & ROOF PLAN

25

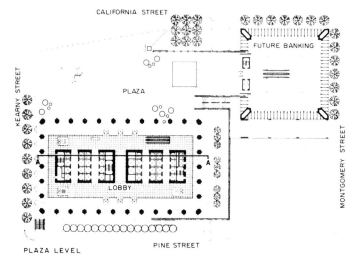

CALIFORNIA STREET

KEARNY STREET

FUTURE BANKING

PLAZA

A ———— A

LOBBY

MONTGOMERY STREET

PLAZA LEVEL

PINE STREET

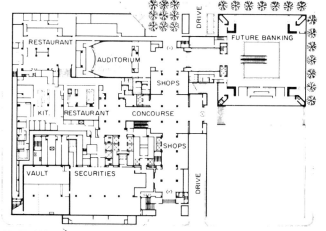

DRIVE

RESTAURANT

AUDITORIUM

FUTURE BANKING

SHOPS

KIT. RESTAURANT CONCOURSE

SHOPS

VAULT SECURITIES

DRIVE

SECTION

CONCOURSE LEVEL

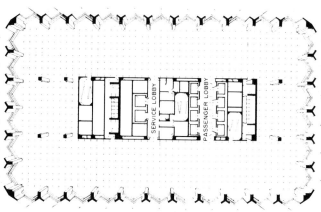

SERVICE LOBBY PASSENGER LOBBY

TYPICAL FLOOR

Roof & Mechanical
Club & Restaurant (51st & 52nd)
Observation Level (50th)

Mechanical Floor (37th)

Mechanical Floor (15th)

International Bank (2nd)
Plaza & Lobby
Concourse Level
Parking & Service
Parking
Parking

steeply sloping site and the extensive planting areas along the street. The placement of the building on the site was influenced by the slope of the site, which falls steeply from Kearny Street on the west to Montgomery Street—San Francisco's Wall Street—on the east. On-site parking was required, and it was put underground (below the concourse level); this dictated, with the sloping site, that the tower be on Pine Street. The main banking offices will be contained in the Phase II portion of the project, a broad, low building now under construction (shaded portion of plan, left).

The tower's color is dark red, with a polished surface that is highly reflective. San Francisco has always been a white city, when seen from any of the hills around it, and as dark buildings begin to appear, the citizens are becoming concerned about their effect on the whole. Both Don Emmons and Pietro Belluschi have given two principal reasons for the building's dark

color. One, white tends to make any object appear larger than it really is and black tends to diminish it. The large building is, in effect, contained by its definite color. Two, it is dark so the windows do not stand out as "holes" in the facade. This allows the walls to be the strong pattern-making element and the tower can be more easily read as a sculptural unity.

The setbacks and the building's profile make window washing an intricate procedure. Belluschi has said this issue influenced several decisions regarding the facade's detailing and its amount of undulation; the solution is certainly ingenious. A W-shaped basic work platform moves up and down the facade within permanent grooves set in the interior corners of the bays. The platform is at all times positively attached to the building, and it is computer controlled—it won't work until all switches are "go". The window-washing system was designed by Manning and Lewis, New Jersey.

The monumental proportions and subtle changes in scale at the base of the tower can be seen best from the plaza side of the block (three photos at left). The International Banking Division of Bank of America occupies the second floor of the tower, and this has been set off from the leased office space above by inverting rather than projecting the windows at the second floor, and making the glass area larger. Inside, this International Banking floor is spacious and dramatic (photo, above).

The detailing of the building is exceptional in its craftsmanship and precision. This can be seen in the transition between wall and window in one plane, in the shape of the octagonal piers at the base, in the way the pier surfaces grow into walls, in the ceiling pattern which reflects the plan, and in the ceiling's carefully integrated downlighting. Such attention to detail is, of course, too rarely found in office buildings these days.

The concourse level of the Bank of America (above, left) shows the imaginative use of lighting to emphasize important crossroads, and again the careful attention to detail. A fortieth-floor executive's office (left) shows how a full bay of the wall system may be used within a partitioning pattern, and the panoramic view it provides.

KNIGHTS OF COLUMBUS BUILDING, New Haven, Connecticut. Architects: *Kevin Roche John Dinkeloo and Associates—David Powrie and Bruce Detmers, project associates.* Mechanical engineers: *Cosentini Associates;* structural engineers: *Pfisterer Tor and Assoc.;* contractor: *Koppers Company, Inc.*

The 23-story tower of the Knights of Columbus Building rises far above the rest of New Haven at the main entrance from the Connecticut Turnpike into the center of town, and seen from the New Haven Railroad terminal four blocks away, it dominates the skyline. Kevin Roche John Dinkeloo & Associates designed the building as this kind of direct entrance event in the city, but it also has a curious relationship to the visual fabric of New Haven itself. As in the photo above, it is a city with several isolated, muscular, sometimes smoking towers jutting up from the lacy and small-scaled fabric of 18th and 19th century residential, academic and commercial architecture around these stacks — industrialization and New England charm side by side. Similarly, the four circular corner shafts of the Knights of Columbus are the strong, muscular parts of the building; vertical, isolated from the whole, carrying the more delicate partially transparent web of steel beams and glass, where the main work of the building is done.

The building itself is simple, and its main components can be

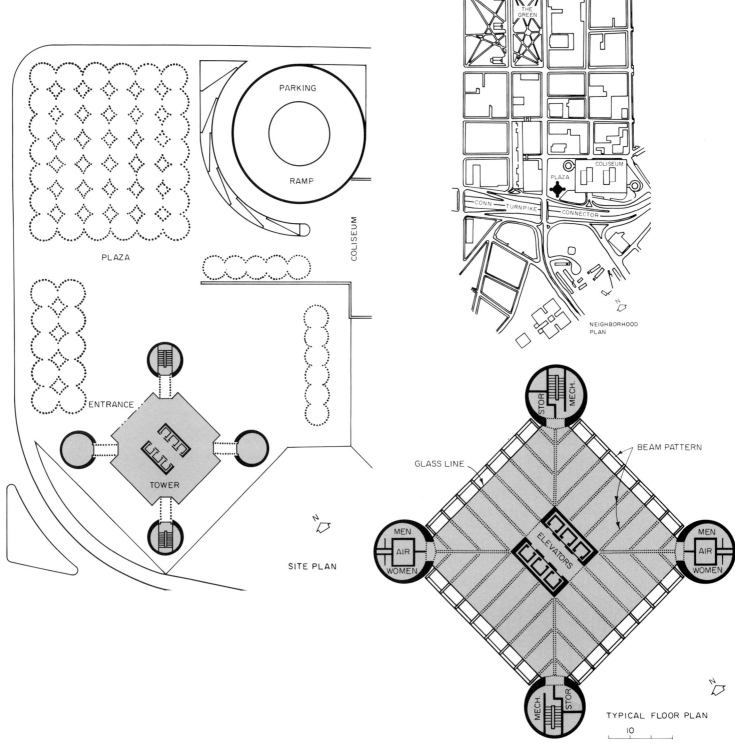

PLAZA

PARKING

RAMP

COLISEUM

ENTRANCE

TOWER

SITE PLAN

THE GREEN

PLAZA

COLISEUM

CONN TURNPIKE

CONNECTOR

NEIGHBORHOOD PLAN

STOR

MECH.

GLASS LINE

BEAM PATTERN

MEN AIR WOMEN

ELEVATORS

MEN AIR WOMEN

MECH. STOR

TYPICAL FLOOR PLAN

10

understood quickly. There are 23 floors, all but three of which are occupied by the national headquarters staff of the Knights of Columbus. The lowest three floors are inset from the rest of the tower, and used as a commercial banking facility plus the entrance lobby. The top floor is mechanical equipment and the fifth floor houses computer facilities for the Knights of Columbus; the other 18 floors are identical clear-span spaces divided by furniture and movable partitions. The core of the tower is occupied by six elevators alone. The two fire stairs re-

quired by code, the lavatories, and the large mechanical equipment spaces are all in the corner towers. These four towers are also the structural supports for the building; they are poured-in-place, post-tensioned concrete, with an ordinary mid-western silo block—13¾ in. x 12⅞ in. x 3¾ in., slightly curved face, natural burn—used as a finishing veneer. The neighboring New Haven Coliseum, also designed by Roche Dinkeloo, is now under construction and has been designed so the two projects will form a compatible whole when complete.

How did the building get this way? Designer's decisions are not very often made in a linear, one-follows-the-other fashion, because the complexities of a problem do not allow it. In retrospect we may see some buildings as evolving from a few simple choices by the architect, however, and this is one. Roche's two basic decisions were that the building be tall and thin rather than low and broad, and that the building express as clearly as possible the material of structural steel with which it would be built. The building grows by rigorously

adhering to and exploiting these two decisions.

A tall building, rather than a shorter, broader one, acknowledges the site as an entrance to the city, as mentioned before, it allows a large and open plaza, and it entirely satisfies the Knights of Columbus' operating methods. The resultant area per floor of a tower on this site—8,000 to 10,000 square feet—is smaller than building economics and efficient use of space normally dictate, however. The core can occupy too large a percentage of the floor area. Consequently, the services nor-

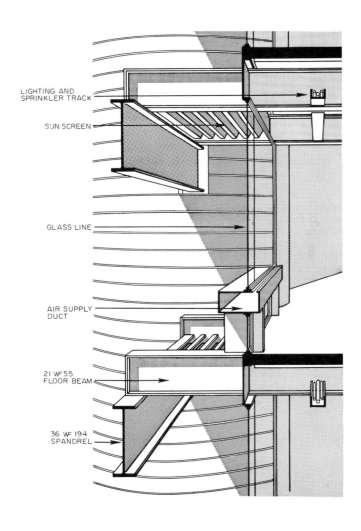

LIGHTING AND
SPRINKLER TRACK

SUN SCREEN

GLASS LINE

AIR SUPPLY
DUCT

21 WF 55
FLOOR BEAM

36 WF 194
SPANDREL

mally found in a core were moved to the exterior, with the exception of the elevators. This relocation allowed the distance from core wall to outside window wall to become 31 feet, adequate for efficient office and aisle layouts within. By retaining the elevators at the center, efficient radiating circulation patterns still remained.

The exposed steel on the tower is exposed *structural* steel, not cover plates or window panels. This is perhaps the only tall office building in the country that has its structural steel uncovered and still passes strin-

gent core-city fire codes. The U.S. Steel building in Pittsburgh does the same thing with water-filled columns, but it is not yet complete. The Ford Foundation building in New York has weathering steel cover plates over conventional insulated beams.

Three design characteristics combined to convince local building inspectors and fire marshals that the exposed beams were safe from heat deformation without insulation. One, the major steel carrying each floor is five feet *outside* the glass line of the building, as in the detail above, center. Re-

cent tests done in Germany, and used by the architects to demonstrate the building's safety, placed steel at various distances outside a glass line or curtain wall, with flames inside, to prove that steel in such locations need not be fireproofed. An added credit was that these tests were performed using smaller steel members than the 36 WF 194 main floor beams of the Knights of Columbus. Large beams dissipate heat more quickly than smaller ones, and are therefore safer, even when loaded to capacity.

Secondly, the major floor

beams bear directly on fireproof concrete that carries straight to the ground. Each silo is fireproof and self-supporting, as is the elevator core in the center; together they are the sole vertical supports for the building. The exits for each floor lead directly into these fireproof shafts, so that the tower may be described as 23 one-story buildings.

Third, the building is sprinkled throughout, which protects deformations in the interior beams. The same exposed weathering steel is also exposed on the inside, and it is a distinct visual asset to the interior

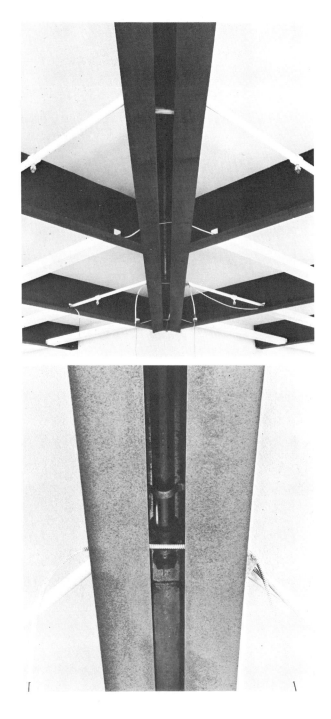

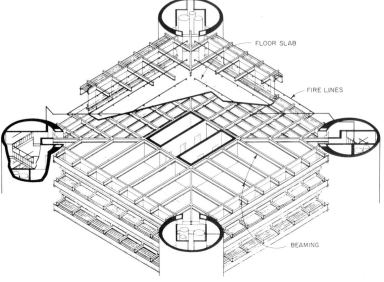

FLOOR SLAB

FIRE LINES

BEAMING

spaces. The two decisions acknowledged originally, then, and the resultant organization of structure and circulation that they caused, can be characterized another way: the building shows a bulldog commitment to the clear visual expression of physical parts, and to the clear visual expression of organization.

Construction and details are critical. To see these general visual commitments through, an architect must be uncompromising in detail decisions; welds and connections may be less

technically direct and efficient than they could be, and construction and erection may become more complex. In this building, the four concrete silos and the elevator core were slip-formed to their full height before any of the floor steel was placed. Each tower is self supporting, and had to be post-tensioned with steel against wind pressure before the towers were connected, so there would be no tension failure in concrete subjected to lateral pressure. The connectors between the tops of the towers in the photo above, left, are the remains of

the slip-form scaffolding; the connectors do not act in any way to tie the towers together before steel is in place.

Many of the beams in the tower rest on frictionless pads so they move with expansion and contraction of the steel. The 36 WF 194 spandrels are subjected to wide temperature variations, being outside the building, and the 21 WF 55 floor framing beams may be expected to expand and contract in an even more unpredictable manner, being partially outside and partially inside the building.

The two small photos above show one of the diagonal beams running from a silo to the core (see framing isometric, left). The beam is two 21 WF 55's placed together, with the sprinkler pipe and main electrical leads running between them. At about five-foot intervals the two beams are pierced, and the secondary sprinkler and electric conduits branch off around the periphery of the building, both concealed by a simple white metal cover channel, seen in the finished interior above. The sprinkler heads can be seen projecting through this cover plate. The lighting is en-

tirely indirect, projected up and reflecting off the concrete under-surface of the floor above, which is painted white. The detailing throughout the building thus remains meticulous and consistent with the architects' commitment to visual expression; each beam reveals itself, each lighting channel carries through, parts are carefully articulated.

The architects also designed all of the furnishings in the building, shown in the photo above and on the next page. The desks, couches and lounge chairs are solid birch

with simple cushions, and are usually fixed in place. The furniture becomes as much a part of the whole as the walls and the spandrel beams: it is an expression of the power of a few simple decisions rigorously applied, and carried through to completion.

The top photo shows a conference room on the twenty-first floor. The middle photo is a typical partition and desk arrangement, showing how the solid partitions work within the beamed ceiling. Below is a view through the elevator core, giving a good feeling for the transparent quality throughout the building. This transparency carries through even to the doors. There are no door jambs, most of each door is made of glass, and there is about one inch of space between doors and frame all the way around. Doors, furniture and partitions were all designed by the architects.

THE FIRST NATIONAL BANK OF CHICAGO, Chicago.
Architects: *C. F. Murphy Associates* and *The Perkins & Will
Partnership.* Interior design for a portion of the plaza level
and for the first and second floors: the joint venture architects,
with personnel from *ISD Incorporated* participating. Interior
design for the Bank's 4th through 21st floors, and the dining
rooms: *Ford & Earl Design Associates—Walter B. Ford II,
principal-in-charge; Robert H. Adams, project coordinator;
Carl Benkert, chief designer.* Acoustics: *Bolt, Beranek &
Newman;* lighting: *Richard Kelly;* contractor: *Gust K.
Newberg Construction Company.*

The First National Bank Tower is a dominating addition to Chicago's commercial architecture, rising
from the very center of the Loop. Along with the
John Hancock Tower and the proposed Sears Roe-
buck Building, it represents a new scale for the city;
it is twice the general height of the older architecture
around it. By 1972 the bank will have a one-half
block plaza in front of it (the old bank building now
adjacent to the new one will be torn down) so that a
different scale of open space will also be introduced
among the existing close buildings and narrow
streets. While these issues of scale hint at the be-
ginnings of a major qualitative change in Chicago's
downtown, other characteristics of the First National
Bank Tower are very much within the city's architectural tradition. It is a skeletal building, acknowledging its structure and its parts in the same manner
as William LeBaron Jenney's Leiter Building of less
than a century ago, or as some of the earlier Chicago
School towers—standing on Dearborn Street with
the First National—still do. The tower's most unusual
feature—its curving slope from base to top—is an
accommodation to several imperatives of circulation
and space. The completed building is a vigor-
ous example of high rise architecture, compatible in its principles with the city's architectural past—and compatible in its dimensions with the city's future.

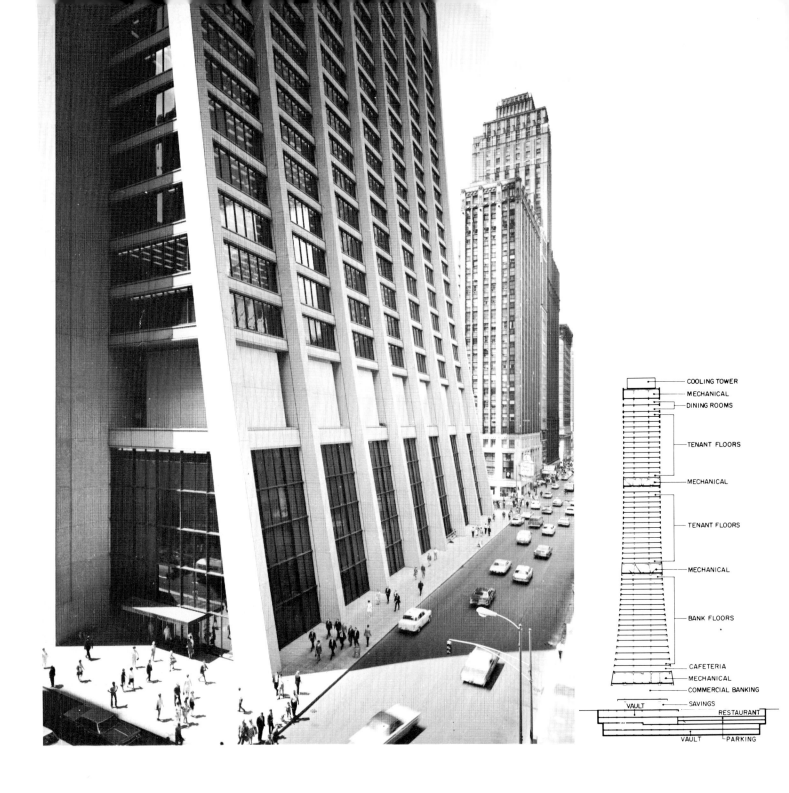

COOLING TOWER
MECHANICAL
DINING ROOMS

TENANT FLOORS

MECHANICAL

TENANT FLOORS

MECHANICAL

BANK FLOORS

CAFETERIA
MECHANICAL
COMMERCIAL BANKING
SAVINGS
VAULT
RESTAURANT
VAULT   PARKING

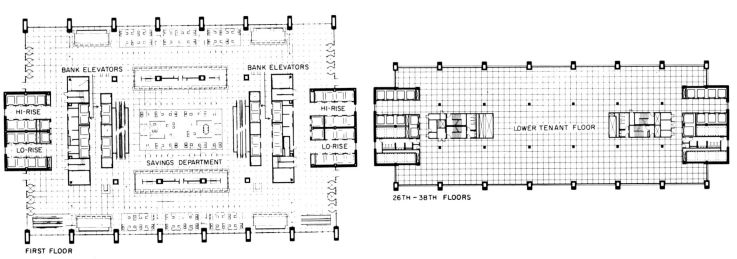

BANK ELEVATORS   BANK ELEVATORS

HI-RISE   HI-RISE

LO-RISE   LO-RISE

SAVINGS DEPARTMENT

LOWER TENANT FLOOR

26TH – 38TH FLOORS

FIRST FLOOR

The curving facade of the bank sweeps directly up from the sidewalk, pressuring the street; the curving wall dominates the scene, looking like a huge ribbed sail caught in the Chicago wind. The surfacing material over the entire building is a soft buff-colored granite; the only material exposed other than this granite is the bronzed glass and the window mullions.

The structural system is steel, and most but not all of the load is carried by the sloping exterior columns, whose visible dimensions are 4.5 feet wide by 12.5 feet long at the ground floor. There are two rows of interior columns in the tower, which can be seen in the section at left, and the vertical loads are redistributed periodically by huge floor-deep trusses at the mechanical equipment floors.

The main banking floor at ground level (photo, above right) occupies the entire base of tower, and the need for this huge room is a principal reason for the building's flare at its base. The First National of Chicago is one of the largest banks in the world, but the state of Illinois does not allow branch banking, so that the First National must do all of its business at this one location. Commercial and small-loan banking is conducted on the mezzanine floating within the main space, with checking, savings, and teller operations on the ground floor. Elevators for the twenty-one floors occupied by the bank itself are on the interior along with the mezzanine escalators, while the upper tenant floor elevators project out at each end of the tower. These outside elevators also lead to the bank's dining rooms on the top two floors. A reception area for one of these dining rooms is shown at right, with its sweeping view of Chicago.

Hedrich Blessing

Balthazar Korab

About half of the interior spaces are occupied by the First National Bank, and about half are leased out to tenants. The materials in the bank interiors are often lush, and designs have been carefully coordinated. Above is one of the 9th floor executive corridors; secretarial and reception areas are partitioned off by transparent floor-to-ceiling plate glass panels, and the material along the long flush wall opposite the elevators is East Indian laurel wood. At the right is a small conference office on the main banking floor, which has been partitioned off from the rest of the space. The floor here is carpeted along with the center portion of the main banking space as a whole. Below is a view of the serving counter in the main employees cafeteria on the fifth floor. The cafeteria seats 550 people, and is heavily used, as all meals for employees are free.

The building is heated and cooled electrically through a hot water system in which boilers have been eliminated. The huge heat transfer machines for the central air conditioning produce hot water in large quantities, which is used in the winter for heat.

Ron Vickers Ltd. photos

TORONTO-DOMINION CENTRE, Toronto, Canada. Owners: *The Toronto-Dominion Bank and Cemp Investments Ltd;* managers: *The Fairview Corporation Limited;* consultant: *Mies van der Rohe;* executive architect: *Sidney Bregman;* architects and engineers: *John B. Parkin Associates and Bregman & Hamann;* structural engineers: *C. D. Carruthers and Wallace Consultants Ltd.;* mechanical and electrical engineers: *H. H. Angus and Associates Ltd.;* lighting consultant: *Edison Price;* general contractor: *Pigott Construction Co. Ltd.;* steel contractor: *Dominion Bridge Co. and Frankel Structural Steel Ltd.;* mechanical contractor: *Crump Mechanical Contracting Ltd.;* electrical contractor: *Ainsworth Canada Ontario-T. D. Project.*

The late works of Ludwig Mies van der Rohe—office towers, high-rise apartments and low pavilions—have all been designed within a stabilized system for each type. Like Doric temples which are also essentially the same, Mies' buildings of the fifties and sixties differ from one another in only the subtlest of ways. Proportions, spatial relationships, the color and texture of chosen materials vary slightly from project to project as modern architecture's most conservative genius painstakingly adjusted them, partially in response to programmatic content but essentially because he believed these elements to be endlessly perfectible in an absolute sense.

Mies' Toronto-Dominion Centre—the last great work in which he took an active part—is a structural and architectural development of ideas which have matured over four decades, and were finally crystallized in New York City's Seagram building (1955-58) and Berlin's New National Gallery (1962-68). The latter, a square pavilion, is similar to the Toronto-Dominion Bank Pavilion, the low element within the complex. The two towers at Toronto are each much larger than the Seagram building. Together they comprise approximately 3.1 million square feet of gross office space as compared to approximately 850,000 square feet in the Seagram.

Because of the size of the Toronto complex and the speed with which it was necessary to erect it (in order to get the office space onto the market and counteract rising building and labor costs), the completion of this project within a reasonable budget, and on time was a major construction management challenge for the team of Canadian architects and engineers who prepared the contract working drawings and supervised construction. (Mies van der Rohe, as consultant, designed the buildings and prepared the preliminary working drawings in collaboration with Dirk Lohan, Bruno Conterato and Joseph Fujikawa, who now head the firm, and Peter Carter, an associate. Sidney Bregman, the executive architect, coordinated the production wing of the team which included John B. Parkin Associates, his own firm of Bregman & Hamann, as well as Canadian structural, mechanical and electrical consultants.) Construction began to advance while the buildings were still in design at a rate which would not have been possible had the Miesian approach not been so steadfast, stabilized, well-tested and clear. In June 1964, six months after the architectural team began work, groundbreaking commenced. By December 1969 the entire complex was complete.

Site, clients and program
Although downtown Toronto was laid out without thought for open spaces or focal points, the completion of Toronto-Dominion Centre marks a change for the better. The new complex is five blocks north of the shore of Lake Ontario and three blocks south of a well-known landmark and the only other focal point —the architecturally controversial new City Hall. Located in a congested area in the midst of such major establishments as the Stock Exchange, brokerage firms, banks and corporate head offices, the Centre occupies a 5½-acre site which has direct vehicular access from three main traffic arteries and is close to suburban rail and subway services.

The mammoth development is a joint venture of the Toronto-Dominion Bank and Cemp Investments Limited. The Bank operates more than 625 branches throughout Canada serving more than 1.5 million Canadians. Cemp Investments Limited is a private investment company owned by trusts created for the children and grandchildren of Canadian industrialist Samuel Bronfman. The latter commissioned Mies van der Rohe and Philip Johnson to design the great Seagram building which Toronto's two new towers closely resemble in detail but not size. (Both Centre towers are considerably bigger.)

Based on a site coverage ratio of 12 to 1, the program called for 3.1 million square feet gross office space to be built in two stages based upon anticipated market demand of 1.7 million and 1.4 million square feet respectively. The program also called for a banking area of 22,500 square feet which would become the headquarters branch of The Toronto-Dominion Bank, replacing their existing premises on the site. To provide attractive downtown facilities for the general public and for the Centre's own working population of 15,000 people, it was decided that the complex should include shops, restaurants, a cinema and underground parking facilities.

Structural and spatial concepts
Mies van der Rohe was convinced that the banking function would require a freer and more flexible type of space than could be provided through incorporating it in an office building. He therefore decided to

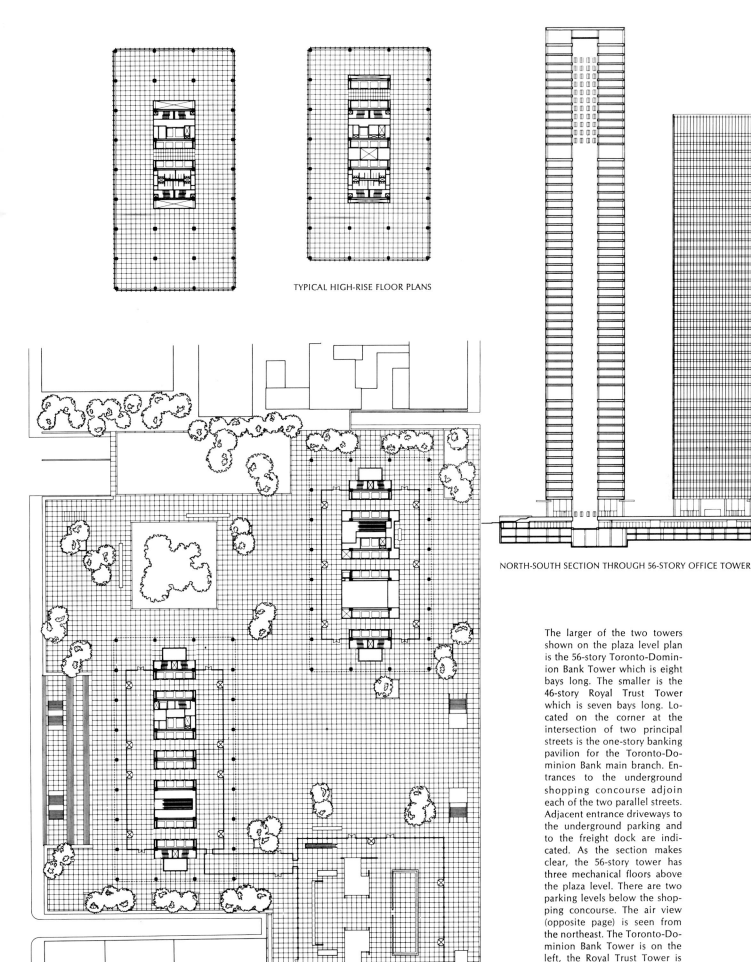

TYPICAL HIGH-RISE FLOOR PLANS

NORTH-SOUTH SECTION THROUGH 56-STORY OFFICE TOWER

The larger of the two towers shown on the plaza level plan is the 56-story Toronto-Dominion Bank Tower which is eight bays long. The smaller is the 46-story Royal Trust Tower which is seven bays long. Located on the corner at the intersection of two principal streets is the one-story banking pavilion for the Toronto-Dominion Bank main branch. Entrances to the underground shopping concourse adjoin each of the two parallel streets. Adjacent entrance driveways to the underground parking and to the freight dock are indicated. As the section makes clear, the 56-story tower has three mechanical floors above the plaza level. There are two parking levels below the shopping concourse. The air view (opposite page) is seen from the northeast. The Toronto-Dominion Bank Tower is on the left, the Royal Trust Tower is on the right and the roof of the Toronto-Dominion Banking Pavilion can be seen in the foreground. Between the two towers people may be seen congregating on the southwest plaza for one of the regular lunchtime concerts.

PLAN AT PLAZA LEVEL

incorporate this complex function in a separate single-story clear span building and to develop the site with this low structure and two office towers in such a way that a number of individually identifiable yet interlinked public plazas would be created at ground level. Because of Toronto's cold climate, he decided that the shopping concourse should be underground, directly beneath the plaza, and above the car parking facility.

The Toronto complex embodies to a high degree at least seven basic Miesian concepts known to all who have carefully studied his work. These concepts may be summarized as follows:

1. Better interpenetration of the spaces between buildings and building elements results from their open, as opposed to closed, placement.

2. A building's magnitude is best established and its range of scales best articulated through a clear expression of the structural system and the components of its construction.

3. The open ground floor, which adds clarification to the structural system, sets a transitional scale between exterior and interior, and by visually and physically uniting plaza and lobby opens one circulation system to another.

4. The introduction of a single-story structure into the larger plaza spaces establishes an intermediate scale gradation between the pedestrian and the bigger spaces.

5. The achievement of a scale range within which the buildings and the outside spaces may be harmoniously related to the human being is of cardinal importance.

6. Landscaping should be used with great care to supplement and complement the interpenetration of space at the pedestrian level and to provide privacy and screening where necessary.

7. The immediate visual and tactile experiences of the pedestrian are greatly enhanced by the use of fine materials and careful detailing for such elements of the plaza as benches, drinking fountains, waste containers, steps, and pools.

Where these concepts have been well realized as in the Toronto-Dominion Centre, the buildings and the spaces between contribute on equal terms towards the creation of a unified environment, restrained yet humane which is at the same time in scale with the city, its traffic and the pedestrian.

Dimensioning the office towers
The dimensions of the structural steel frame and the building module were influenced by the following factors:

1. A structural bay of 30- by 40-feet accommodates the required

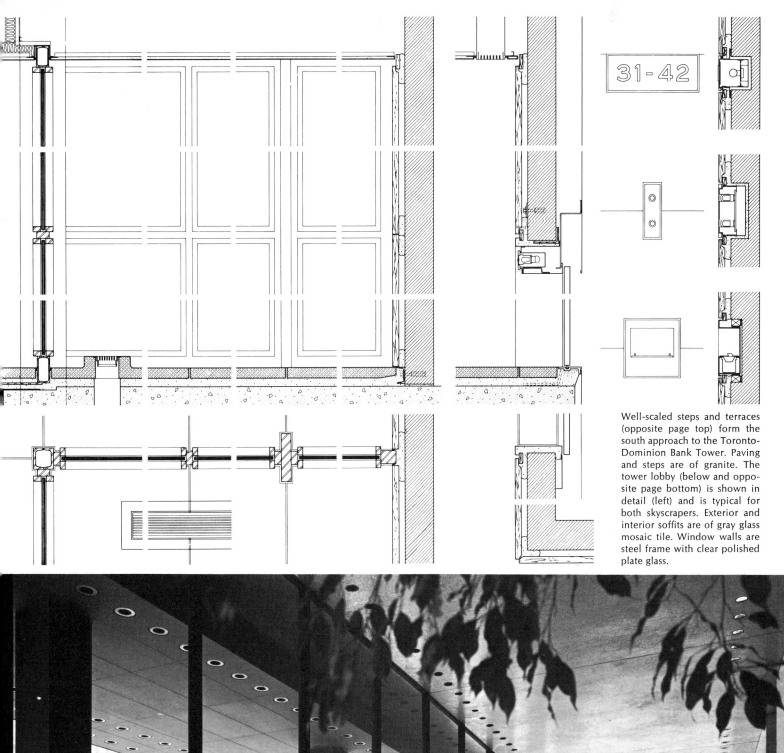

31-42

Well-scaled steps and terraces (opposite page top) form the south approach to the Toronto-Dominion Bank Tower. Paving and steps are of granite. The tower lobby (below and opposite page bottom) is shown in detail (left) and is typical for both skyscrapers. Exterior and interior soffits are of gray glass mosaic tile. Window walls are steel frame with clear polished plate glass.

elevators, stairs and toilets, which together with the building's service ducts, form the central tower cores.

2. The 40-foot dimension affords column-free peripheral office space, thus permitting optimum layouts throughout the complete range of tenant space requirements. Toronto-Dominion Centre's management figures that the absence of free-standing columns in the office spaces due to the 30- by 40-foot bay provides a 15 per cent saving in office area and a 5 per cent increase in employee efficiency—a total rental saving of over $2.00 per sq. ft.

3. The subdivision of the 30- by 40-foot structural bay into 5-foot modular increments provides the most reasonable degree of flexibility for a building of multiple tenancies. This module sets the dimensions of the ceiling elements, including the combined fluorescent light and air handling fixtures; the peripheral induction units; and the location of the vertical mullion divisions of the buildings' skin.

4. The 12-foot floor to floor height of the structural frame is determined by a clear floor to ceiling dimension of 9 feet plus a floor depth of 3 feet—the minimum needed to accommodate structural steel beams and girders, decking, floor and ceiling finishes and air conditioning, lighting and electrical services.

5. At the plaza level the clear floor to soffit height is 26 feet—a vertical dimension in proportional accord with the size of the public entrance lobby space.

Curtain wall details for towers

The elevation (top right) indicates the skin details for the roof, typical office floors and the second floor above the lobby level. The mullion detail (middle) shows the typical dry-wall partition to be located anywhere within the 5-foot-module, the extruded aluminum glazing frame with bronze-gray tinted heat-absorbing and glare-reducing glass, and the built-up steel mullion unit. The typical corner detail (bottom) shows the induction unit, the glass and its frame, dry-wall fire insulation around the column, the steel mullion and corner cover unit and the light-weight concrete back-up. The skin details (far right) include: a section through the roof (top) which shows the steel cap angle, the insulation and built-up roofing surfaced with black granite chips, the steel mullion and spandrel plate, the light-weight concrete and the extruded aluminum frame and louvers; a typical floor section with a vertical expansion joint which indicates the perforated metal pan ceiling and the venetian blind detail; and a section at the second floor level showing the gray glass mosaic tile soffit.

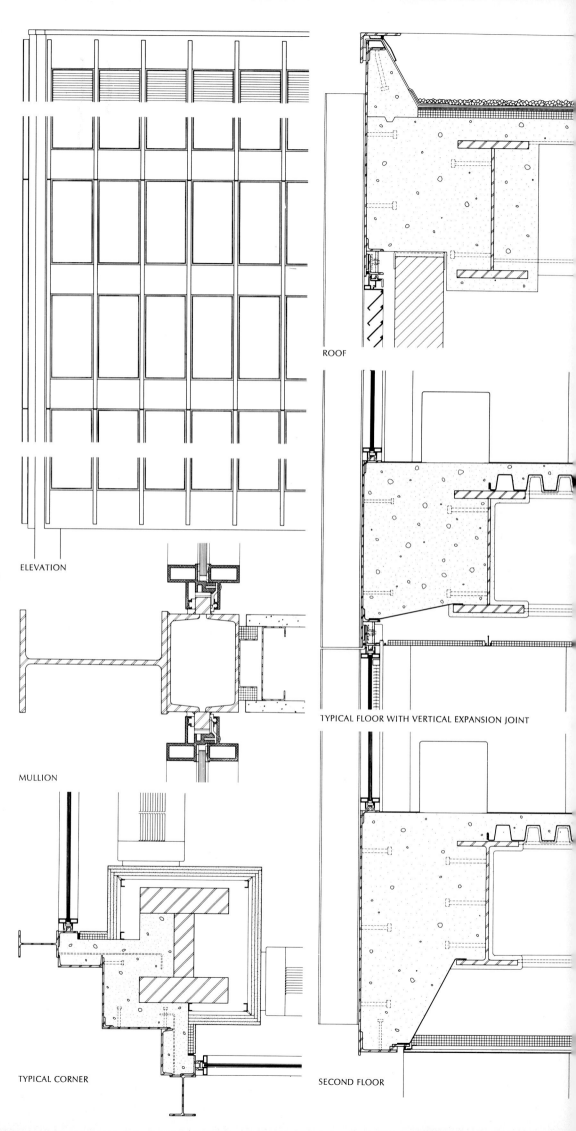

ELEVATION

MULLION

TYPICAL CORNER

ROOF

TYPICAL FLOOR WITH VERTICAL EXPANSION JOINT

SECOND FLOOR

The steel mullions, spandrel plates and column covers are painted matte black. The extruded aluminum glazing frame has a matte baked finish.

The photographs (opposite, top and below) taken in the Toronto-Dominion Bank executive suite on the 54th floor of the 56-story office tower indicate that the curtain wall proportions are as handsome on the interior as they are on the exterior.

Tower structural design, fabrication and erection

The 56-story Toronto-Dominion Bank Tower is three 40-foot bays wide by eight 30-foot bays long; the 46-story Royal Trust Tower is three 40-foot bays wide by seven 30-foot bays long. Typically, a bay consists of 40-foot long girders at 30-foot centers (spanning the transverse direction) and 30-foot long intermediate beams at 10-foot centers (spanning the longitudinal direction). The steel frame of the towers utilizes a braced core system in both the transverse and longitudinal directions. In the transverse direction, a K-bracing system extending the full tower height was developed on four interior column lines and other interior transverse bents have core bracing up to the floor where the elevator banks terminate. In the longitudinal direction the vertical rigidity of the core is developed by a combination of inverted knee braces in some bays and moment resisting beam-to-column connections in others. Since the core was still not stiff enough to satisfy the maximum sway limitations of .002 times the building height, a system of cantilever trusses was introduced at each of the towers' lower 24-foot-high mechanical floors—extending from the core to the perimeter columns—in order to make the total building width effective against overturning. The 56-story tower was designed to deflect no more than 12 inches in a steady 100-mph wind. The stiffening provided actually limits sway to between 6 and 8 inches.

The installation of the first 43 stories of steel skin for the 56-story tower was by the "stick" method, i.e., fascia plates were attached to edge beams followed by the welding to them of individual two-story-high mullions. Because this system proved to have a number of disadvantages, a "panel" method of installation was substituted from the 44th floor up as well as for the subsequent 46-story tower. This method involved the setting up on the site of a jig capable of holding the spandrel and mullion components of a two-story (24-foot-high) steel skin panel six or eight modules wide. After welding, the unpainted areas of the panel were prime-coated while still in the jig. When panels for one complete floor had been fabricated, derricks were used to lift them into position.

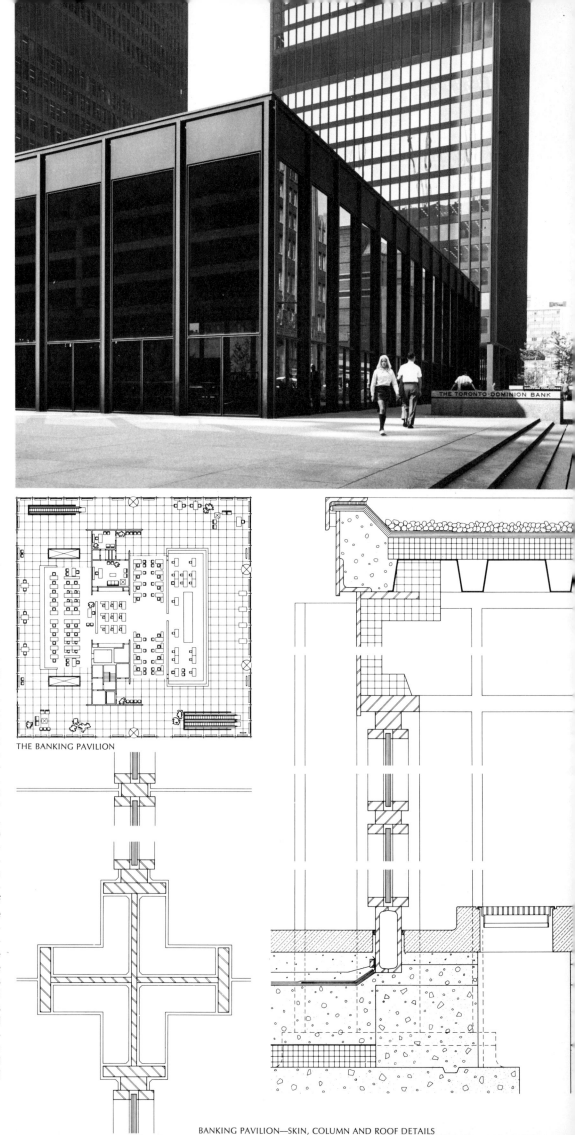

THE BANKING PAVILION

BANKING PAVILION—SKIN, COLUMN AND ROOF DETAILS

BANKING PAVILION—SKIN AND CEILING DETAILS

The banking pavilion

The main branch of the Toronto-Dominion Bank (shown in photos, plan and details right) is housed in the single story, 150-foot-square, clear span, steel and glass pavilion located at the principal corner of the site. This pavilion is identical in size and shape to Mies' Berlin Museum, except for the museum's overhanging roof. The principal customer services such as the teller, credit and savings departments are located at the plaza level, while securities, safety deposit and other functions are accommodated directly below at the concourse level.

The roof structure of the banking pavilion consists of a two-directional system comprising 4 feet 6 inches deep steel girders and diaphragm beams at 10-foot centers, each supported at the periphery by steel columns of cruciform shape.

The air conditioning of the pavilion is accomplished by peripheral floor supply outlets working in conjunction with centrally positioned units on the top of the two wood panelled cores. Air is extracted through openings located on the south face of the two marble-faced mechanical shafts. These shafts also accommodate air intake ducts from the roof, rain water pipes and electrical services.

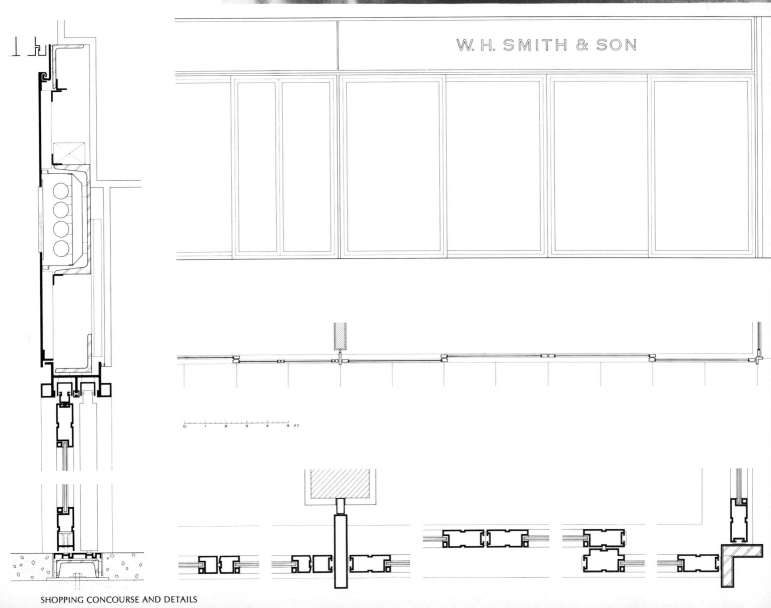

W. H. SMITH & SON

SHOPPING CONCOURSE AND DETAILS

NAGAKIN CAPSULE TOWER BUILDING, Tokyo, Japan. Architect: *Kisho Noriaki Kurokawa;* structural engineers: *Gengo Matsui and ORS.* General contractor: *Taisei Construction Co. Ltd.*

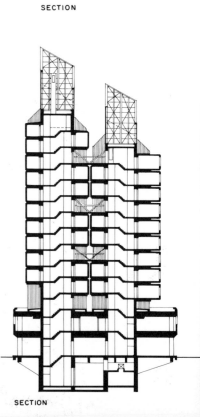

SECTION

Each of the little boxes shown being hoisted into place is now occupied by a single individual, usually an executive on a business trip to Tokyo. As the photo (overleaf) indicates, the total complex is now finished, all of the 140 capsules are now in place and every one of them has been sold. The buyers, individuals or corporations, paid prices ranging from 13,000– 16,000 dollars, depending on the capsule's location within the complex and the quality of its interior finishes and fittings. The total construction cost of the Nakagin Capsule Tower Building, including all the capsules was $1.2-million. The entire complex provides general housekeeping and hotel services, and judging from the speed with which the units have been sold, is ideal for the needs of the Japanese business man. The first floor of the complex consists of an entrance lobby and a restaurant. Business offices for capsule owners are located on the second floor. The capsules are attached in the form of a spiral to two towers of a steel-frame and rein-forced-concrete rigid-frame structure. The capsules are of lightweight steel frame covered with panels of galvanized steel. Air conditioning within the individual capsules is provided by means of a fan coil unit. The general contractor for the entire complex was Taisei Construction Co. Ltd. Structural design was by Gengo Matsui and the ORS office. Planning for disaster protection (mainly the prevention and detection of fire) was done by Kurokawa's office in collaboration with the Hoshino Laboratory.

SECTION

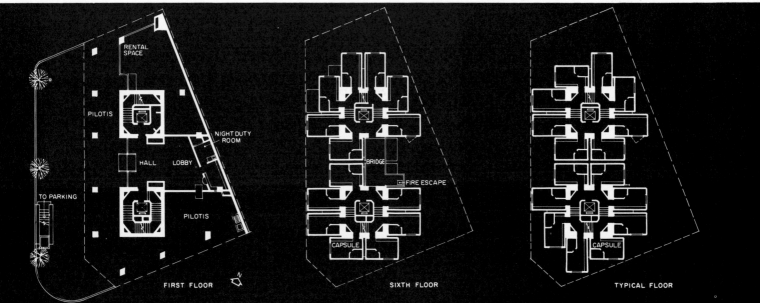

FIRST FLOOR   SIXTH FLOOR   TYPICAL FLOOR

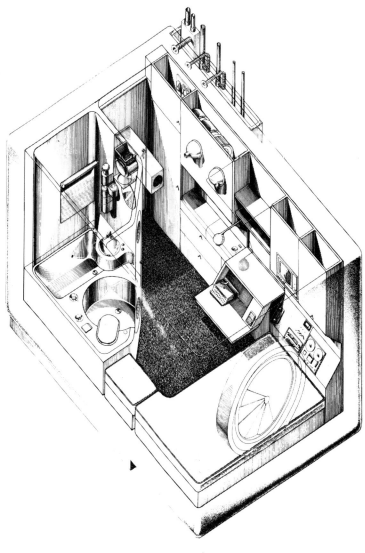

Capsule furniture was manufactured in units. It includes a closet, the air-conditioning unit, desk unit, overhead console unit and a bed. The fan coil unit is fitted into the upper part of the air-conditioning unit, and the lower portion is used for storage. The refrigerator and sink are optional. Storage is provided above and below the desk, and a portion of the bed can be pulled out and used as a chair. The overhead console unit doubles as a headboard for the bed. It may include audio-visual equipment.

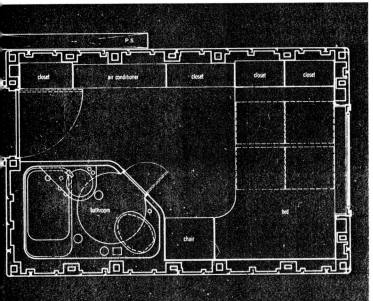

CBS-GATEWAY TOWER, St. Louis, Missouri. Architects: *Hellmuth, Obata and Kassabaum, Inc.—Gyo Obata, principal-in-charge of design; Herbert J. Koopman, project architect; Terry F. Cashen, project designer; Michael D. Tatum, Michael L. Willis and Kenneth H. Hanser, interior design group;* structural engineers: *The Engineers Collaborative;* mechanical engineers: *William Tao & Associates;* acoustical engineers: *Paul S. Veneklasen & Associates.*

Gateway Tower occupies a choice location in St. Louis' downtown redevelopment area, overlooking Gateway Arch and the river—a situation the developer sought to enhance through design of a quality calculated to lure top tenants.

The building is composed of a block-long three-story wing devoted to radio and television studios and related offices for CBS, the principal tenant, and at one end a nineteen-story office tower designed to take full advantage of the sweeping views via glass walls and cantilevered balconies on three sides.

Morley Baer photos

In the studio wing, offices are ranged along the street side of the building to afford them an outside view and to buffer the studios from traffic noise. Two levels of underground parking are provided below.

In the tower, vertical circulation, and mechanical and service space are concentrated along the western elevation and in a compact central core, leaving the bulk of each floor free for interior space arrangement according to the needs of individual tenants. In a typical office suite (above) designed by HOK, areas not requiring outside exposure are grouped on the interior, and offices paired at the perimeter with each pair sharing a secretarial area, so that all occupied spaces are open to light and view.

Both building elements are of reinforced concrete, sandblasted to expose the beige aggregate.

Eugene H. Fleming III

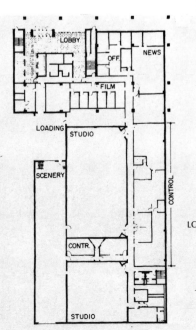

LOBBY LEVEL

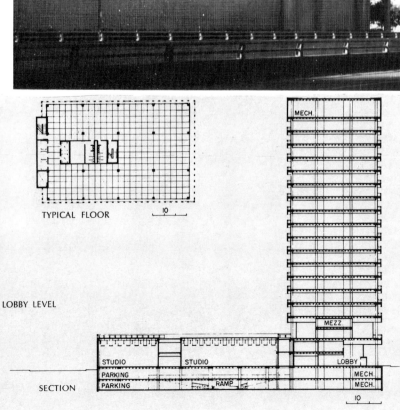

TYPICAL FLOOR

SECTION

BUREAU OF RECLAMATION ENGINEERING & RESEARCH CEN-
TER, Denver, Colorado. Architects: *Hellmuth, Obata and Kassabaum, Inc.—Gyo Obata, principal-in-charge of design; Rolf
Muenter, project manager; Chih-Chen Jen and Robert E. Ed-
monds, project designers; associate architects: Scott Associates;
structural engineers: Ketchum, Konkel, Ryan & Fleming; mechanical engineer: Harold P. Brehm.*

The powerfully rendered headquarters for the
Bureau of Reclamation, at fourteen stories the
tallest structure in Denver's growing Federal
Center, consists of a twelve-story office block
rising from a plaza which roofs ancillary facilities
grouped on the ground floor.

Designed on an extremely tight schedule,
(five months from contract to bid documents)
the building nevertheless came in substantially
below estimate, thanks in large part to the clearly
detailed structural system which also imparts to
the building its interior flexibility and the strong
textural quality of its façade.

Julius Shulman photos

Because sun glare at Denver's high altitude is unusually intense, windows were recessed three feet and shielded by precast concrete sunscreens which produce a rich rhythmic pattern on the building exterior. On the interior, the prestressed concrete structure provides 40-foot clear spans on either side of the 30-foot-wide central core, assuring flexibility of space configuration on the office floors. The coffered slab, exposed throughout the tower portion of the building, forms finished ceiling and housing for lighting fixtures.

In addition to offices for executive staff, and the research and engineering departments, the tower houses a library and computer center. The ground floor houses the employee cafeteria, reproduction facilities (including darkrooms and print rooms), and mechanical equipment.

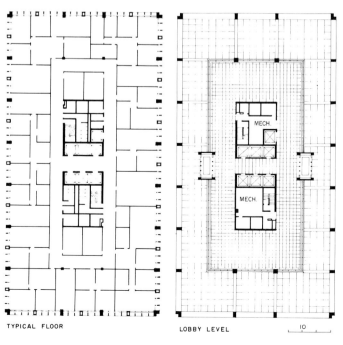

TYPICAL FLOOR

LOBBY LEVEL

AVENUE OF THE STARS OFFICE BUILDING, Century City, Los Angeles, California. Architects: *Hellmuth, Obata and Kassabaum, Inc.*—*Gyo Obata,* principal-in-charge of design; *King Graf,* project manager; *Jerome J. Sincoff,* project architect; *James R. Henrekin,* project designer; associate architects: *Charles Luckman Associates;* structural engineers: *The Engineers Collaborative, S. B. Barnes & Associates;* mechanical engineers: *Ayres & Hayakawa;* electrical engineer: *Michael J. Garris.*

A new addition to the Aluminum Company of America's distinguished Century City development, which also includes a major hotel, apartments, and several other office buildings, this sleek 20-story tower provides quarters for corporate offices and professional firms with varying requirements as to size and configuration of space. To accommodate this multi-tenant occupancy, the 100-by-240-foot tower floors consist of wholly unobstructed space distributed about a central service-circulation core, achieving an efficiency ratio of 82 per cent.

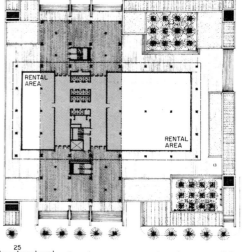

25

Rental areas penetrating the tower lobby at plaza level are occupied by a branch bank and an investment brokerage house, while a four-level garage below grade provides tenants off-street parking space.

The steel frame structure is sheathed in a bronze hard anodic aluminum skin which is made of flat and bent sheet and extruded sections in sizes as large as 5 by 10 feet, and punctuated by bold squares of floor-to-ceiling glass.

FORD FOUNDATION BUILDING, New York City. Architects: *Kevin Roche John Dinkeloo and Associates—associates: Eugene Festa, Philip Kinsella,* and *(for interior furnishings) Warren Plattner;* structural engineers: *Severud Associates;* mechanical engineers: *Cosentini Associates;* acoustical consultant: *Michael J. Kodaras;* landscape architect: *Dan Kiley;* general contractor: *Turner Construction Company.*

By enclosing a third of an acre garden in walls of glass twelve stories high, the architects of the Ford Foundation Building, Kevin Roche John Dinkeloo and Associates, have created a new kind of urban space that stands between the sealed environment of a modern office building and the increasingly harsh and uncontrolled urban landscape outside.

Original architectural ideas are rare and hard to come by; and, when they appear, they usually set off a train of related developments. While the Ford Foundation building is very much one of a kind, a special case, it is directly related to problems of the urban environment that architects and planners everywhere are trying to solve.

When architects come to visit the Ford Foundation Building, however, they are going to get a surprise. While the basic concept of the building may seem simple enough in drawings and photographs, in actuality it is tremendously complex and paradoxical. The design, which might be expected to produce a sense of informality, openness and candor, is actually highly charged with a symbolic content that invests the most ordinary aspects of the building's life with an almost ritualistic significance.

One does not simply drive up to the Ford Foundation, but approaches it by a carefully planned processional way, which turns the mundane requirements of a one-way street system into a ceremonial journey of surprise and discovery. Traffic regulations require that every car headed for the 43rd Street entrance to the Ford Foundation must first drive east on 41st Street, and turn left on to Tudor City Place, which crosses 42nd Street on a bridge, affording a highly interesting three-quarter view of the Foundation building. The building is not visible again until the car pulls into the entrance-way of the 43rd Street facade, a closed composition of granite and glass which affords no hint of the light and spacious garden court within.

This sequence, rather reminiscent of a slide lecture by Vincent Scully describing the approach to a Greek temple, is not an accident but conscious contrivance. In the same way, the Ford Foundation building itself is far more than office space for some 350 employees. It is a symbolic statement that seems to characterize the Foundation's relation to the world around it, and the relationship of its employees to each other.

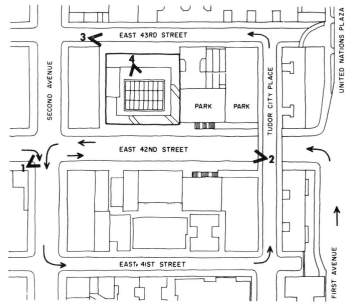

To the visitor arriving by automobile the building bursts into view suddenly at a turn in the tortuous one-way street system . . .

The main entrance, once reached, is dark and cave-like, then opens to a slowly unfolding vista of the lofty interior garden . . .

Roche was certain from the beginning that he should not create a typical New York office building, which he calls just a multiplication of ground floor space. He also felt that the Foundation, which has grown very rapidly over the past 10 years, suffered from a lack of communication and needed to be housed in a building strongly expressive of relationship and the organization's personality.

The site is an unusual one, near the United Nations Building, at the east end of 42nd Street, one of Manhattan's most prominent cross-town streets. The plot selected by the Foundation is not prominent in itself, however; it is not large and does not occupy a corner. The most salient characteristic of the location is its proximity to Tudor City, a self-contained group of apartment houses dating from around 1930, whose frosting of Elizabethan detail gives the complex its name. Tudor City's main level is more than a story above 42nd Street, and two parks at this upper level adjoin the Ford site's eastern edge.

Roche knew that a courtyard of some kind would be an important part of his design, but his initial concept was an L-shaped building with a stepped section that terraced down to meet the space of the Tudor City parks. The decision to reach out and enclose the courtyard space established the basic concept, and the rest of the building follows logically from it. The courtyard still steps up an entire story from 42nd to 43rd Street, and several of the lower floors of the building still step back to create terraces; but the interior volume becomes a single space, and pulls the whole building together in a very powerful way. The court becomes a park, which is open to the public and is a tremendously generous gift to the city, as is the care and restraint with which the building's dimensions, proportions and colors have been related to its neighbors. The warm tones of the granite facing and the rust-surfaced steel harmonize particularly well with the red brick of Tudor City.

The offices are grouped around the court in such a way that it provides both a physical and visual transition between the office space and the world outside. The court serves as a giant return for the conditioned air supplied to the offices, and the offices and corridors that look out on the court have doors that can be opened and slid back. The court also provides a variety of outlook and a constant point of reference. Roche speaks of it as a "living room" for the whole Foundation that provides a sense of community for everyone who works there. The sense of community is certainly present, but the visitor is likely to find that "living room" is too domestic a term. In fact, the space is little short

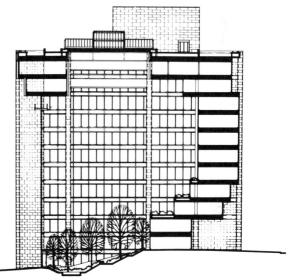

The interior courtyard pulls the building together in a very powerful way and forms a new kind of urban experience, a park whose climate is controlled, and where flowers bloom all year around . . .

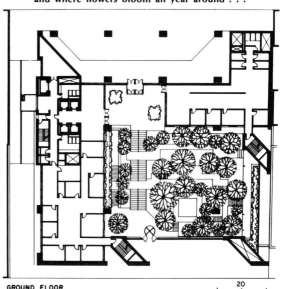

GROUND FLOOR   20

of awe-inspiring, and the sense of organization that is projected is one of ritual, hierarchy, and immense power.

It is difficult to say why this effect should have occurred. One reason may be that, by enclosing the court, Roche has made the entire building essentially four-square; that is, the building's height, length and width are very similar. The four-square building with an interior court is a traditional symbolic representation of the universe, and as such is an ancient symbol of power, used in religious buildings and palaces. The palace of the king of kings, the temple of the New Jerusalem, the house of the world, are the concepts this shape connotes.

Whatever the reason, the most ordinary aspects of the Foundation building seem charged with special significance. For example, it is very typical corporate symbolism for the top floor to be the executive floor; so typical, in fact, that one ceases to think of this arrangement as symbolic. But, in the Ford Foundation building, the president is visibly above everyone else; one can look up and see him from virtually every point in the building. Not only that, but directly above *his* head is the office of the Chairman of the Board, whose office is the only one adjoining the court that does not look out on it. The two offices seem to become the visible and invisible manifestations of a mysterious power.

The building consists of executive suites, as the non-executive work of the Foundation is contracted out, through the medium of grants. Each office is done in the same rich palette of subdued natural materials. To the outsider, all the offices appear identical, and the activity of the occupants thus completely unintelligible. The visitor senses, however, that, to the initiate, the fine gradation of office location and sizes has a definite meaning; so that, seeing all, he knows he is excluded. A final symbolic note is struck by the fact that almost all the metal trim in the building is brass; that is, one knows it is brass, but actually one thinks of it as solid gold, the ancient perquisite of priests and kings. The pervasiveness of gold elevates everything to the status of cult object. Telephones, filing cabinets, typewriter stands, door trim, stair rails, all appear to be of solid gold. Most striking of all are three golden brass doors that lie at the end of a precipitous descent into the basement.

If the building has acquired a symbolic life of its own, however, it is because the Ford Foundation gave its architects the freedom—and the money—to make the design a work of art. And if the result has the effect of picking out and over-emphasizing certain aspects of the Founda-

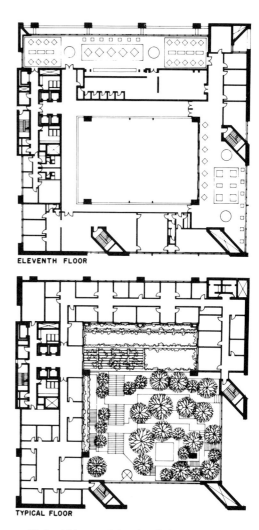

ELEVENTH FLOOR

TYPICAL FLOOR

All furnishings and interior fittings (opposite)
are done in the same rich palette
of subdued natural materials.
All metal trim is brass, but seems to be solid gold.
Straight and narrow stair (below)
leads to conference and board rooms.

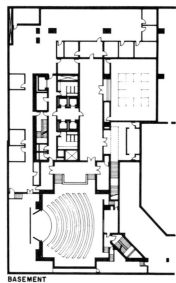

BASEMENT

tion's organizational character, it is because the design has a tremendous symbolic power that no one could have anticipated before it was built. It is, perhaps, the most important contribution of this building that it demonstrates that a space only modern technology makes possible can command an almost archaic significance.

The experience of the court is also an important one. The design of landscape architect, Dan Kiley, has made it a real garden, and not just a collection of potted plants. In a time of rapidly increasing urbanization, growing densities, and a more and more frenetic pace of life, a garden court of this kind becomes an oasis of tranquility and a point of balance in an uncertain world.

Thus, the design of the Ford Foundation Building, although unique, is also suggestive, and it will be interesting to see if it will have an influence on other buildings. One certainly hopes it will.

Golden doors (below) lead to auditorium-conference room

Alexandre Georges photos

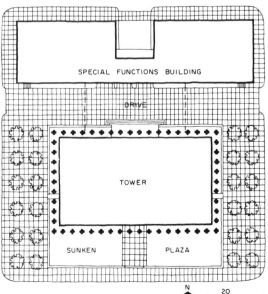

SPECIAL FUNCTIONS BUILDING

DRIVE

TOWER

SUNKEN   PLAZA

N   20

ELECTRIC TOWER, Houston. Owner: *Houston Lighting & Power Company.* Architects: *Wilson, Morris, Crain & Anderson—Robert O. Biering, associate architect;* structural engineers: *Walter P. Moore & Associates;* landscape architect: *Fred Buxton & Associates;* lighting consultant: *Edison Price;* acoustical consultant: *Dr. Paul Boner;* contractor: *W. S. Bellows Construction Company.*

Wilson, Morris, Crain & Anderson have provided downtown Houston's fast-changing cityscape with the handsome 27-story tower shown in detail above, as part of a trim solution to both the general office and special computer-oriented needs of their client, Houston Lighting & Power Company. The architects rejected the obvious, though economical, solution of filling the 250-foot-square block of real estate with a single six-to-eight-story building. Instead, a low windowless computer center is linked to a 27-story office tower, which, as pictured on these pages, creates a strong image on both skyline and street, shows off the company's services in a skillful integration of heating, lighting and architecture, and as an added bonus, offers as a public garden what it saved in land.

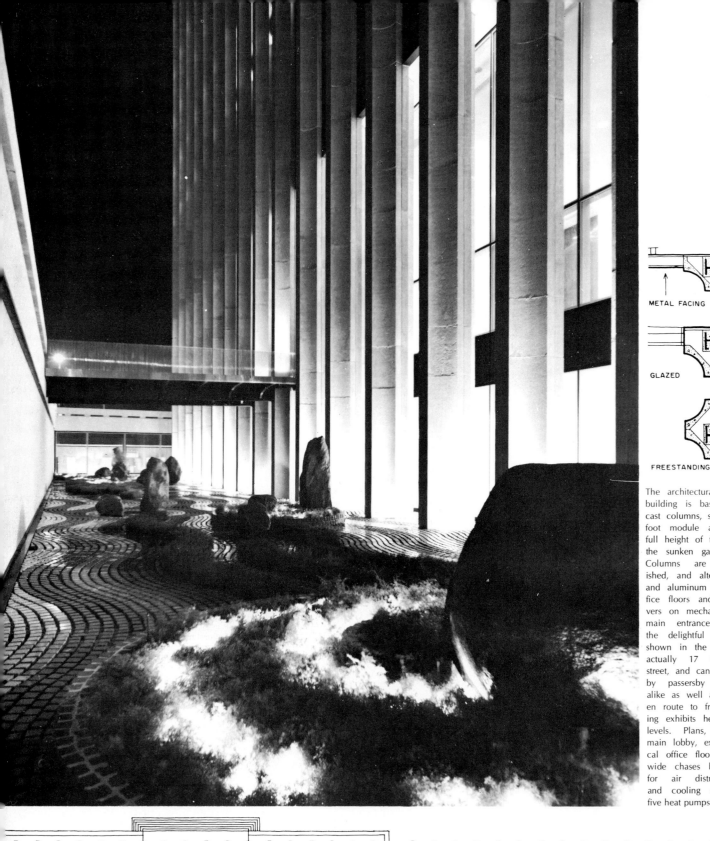

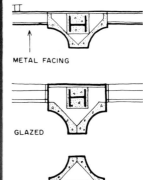

METAL FACING

GLAZED

FREESTANDING

The architectural theme for the building is based on the pre-cast columns, spaced on a five-foot module and carrying the full height of the building from the sunken garden shown left. Columns are aggregate finished, and alternate with glass and aluminum spandrels on office floors and aluminum louvers on mechanical floors. The main entrance bridge crosses the delightful Japanese garden shown in the photo, which is actually 17 feet below the street, and can thus be enjoyed by passersby and employees alike as well as by the visitors en route to frequent homemaking exhibits held on the lower levels. Plans, below, include main lobby, executive and typical office floors. The unusually wide chases house dual ducts for air distribution. Heating and cooling are provided by five heat pumps on top floor.

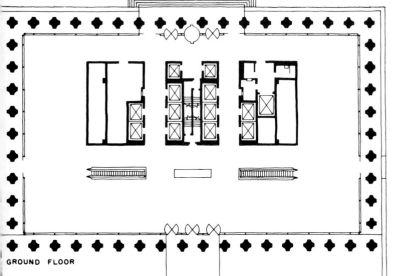

GROUND FLOOR

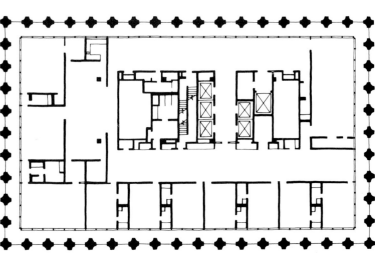

EXECUTIVE FLOOR

Main lobby and garden lobby (right) provide ample public exhibit space, while floors above are solely for company use. "Programmers' bridge" below, linking tower and annex, spans company car drive, main lobby and below-grade garage entrances. Heavy paper flow is processed in annex, routed via separate truck docks to stay clear of drive.

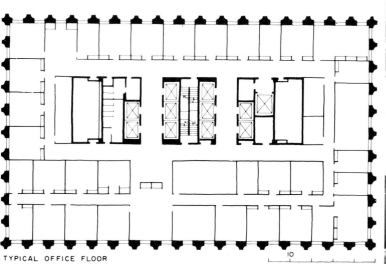

TYPICAL OFFICE FLOOR   10

Executive floor elevator lobby, above, leads to reception area, right. Offices here, as throughout, make good use of advanced mechanical concepts. Heat-from-light, for example, is returned for redistribution through slots in special fluorescent luminaires, shown in office below. The fixture itself was designed for open parabolic-louvered low brightness and minimal glare, yet with high foot-candles and efficiency. Lighting and materials complement each other throughout. Neutral teak and marble are accented in brilliantly colored furniture and felt walls. Wall in office below is formed by half-columns, while office to right is inset for continuous glazing. Special glazing includes outer, open-ended glass panels, to promote convection currents for cooling in summer. Draft barrier strip heaters line windows.

Columns and spandrels of exterior tower walls taper from 4 feet 6 inches at second floor level (with an additional taper at the base) to 12 inches at top. There are no interior columns: in each tower, the main beams, I-shaped and spaced 10 ft. o.c., span 42 feet clear. The 28-story building is of reinforced concrete throughout, sandblasted both inside and out.

MACMILLAN BLOEDEL BUILDING, Vancouver, British Columbia, Owner: *MacMillan, Bloedel, Ltd.* Architects: *Erickson/Massey and Francis Donaldson —Arthur Erickson, partner-in-charge of design; James Strasman, project architect for Erickson/Massey; Procter Lemare, project architect, production, for Francis Donaldson;* structural engineer: *Otto Safir;* mechanical, electrical engineers; *Reid Crowther & Partners, Ltd.;* soils engineers: *R. A. Spence, Ltd.;* special lighting consultants: *William M. C. Lam & Associates;* acoustics consultants: *Bolt, Beranek, and Newman, Inc.;* graphics consultants: *Lester Beall & Associates;* contractor: *Laing Construction & Equipment, Ltd.*

The new MacMillan Bloedel building in Vancouver, British Columbia, is the latest— and finest—building of the young firm of Erickson/Massey, whose principals gained international fame a few years ago with their winning design for Simon Fraser University. This new office building, their first tall building—urbane, well suited to its location and well sited in the downtown part of the city, and much the reflection of itself which the client wanted—almost did not come into being.

MacMillan Bloedel Limited, Canada's largest forest products company, had considered a number of proposals for a headquarters building. Finally, unhappy with the then latest, (a package deal for a typical core-plan building with a precast curtain wall) they first asked Erickson/Massey to improve, then to restudy their entire pro-

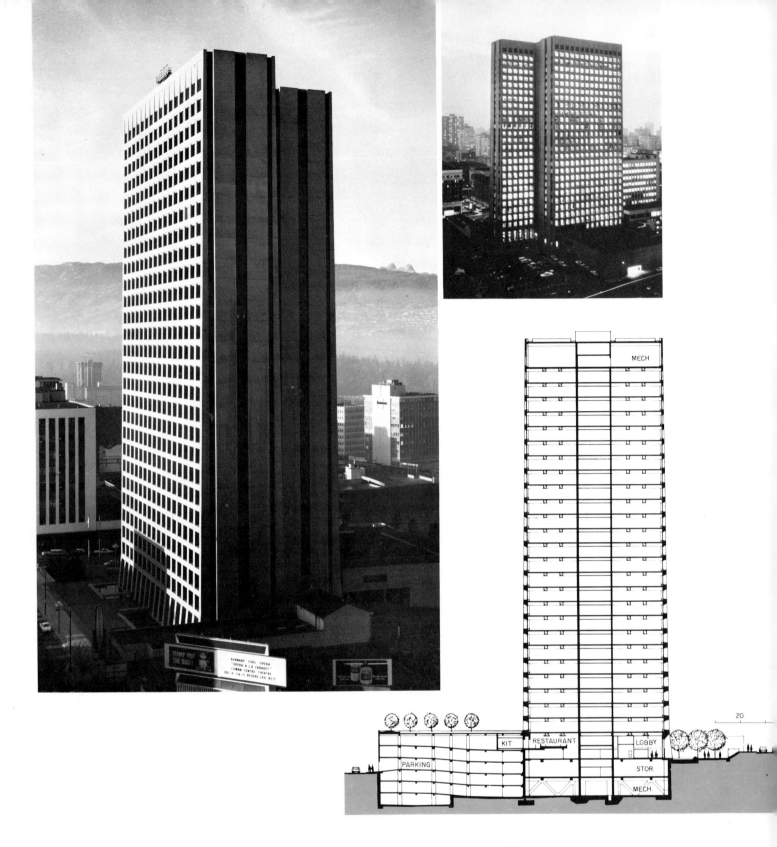

gram and suggest—in two months—an equally economical but architecturally distinctive solution. In the specified time the architects produced a design for the building based on one pervading concept, simplicity: outside, giving expression to the "vigor, directness and strength" which the architects found characteristic of their clients' company; and inside, reducing the usual office clutter by minimizing the number of elements needed for good function.

This elegant leanness is best described in Arthur Erickson's own words: "a Doric building in its starkness and simplicity." This is nowhere more evident than in the exterior wall surface, the most important feature of the building. Its concrete, un-

relieved except for the square opening of the deep-set windows, reads as it was poured, says Erickson, "because the total surface is big enough for the irregularities to act as a patina to the concrete." The size of the openings was carefully calculated to let the wall act as a wall, not as a system of spandrels and columns (which is the structural solution) and to permit the use of one sheet of glass, unbroken by mullion or muntin, in each opening. The effect is, to quote Erickson again, "of glass jammed into the concrete directly to bring out the extreme contradiction of character of each. All detail was avoided in achieving an uncompromising junction between glass and concrete—void and solid."

Floodlighting at night dramatically emphasizes the "contradiction of void and solid" and the concrete nature of the building. The sunken plaza along the building front affords a view of the venerable Hotel Vancouver and a picturesque contrast in architectural style and statement. The building is entered across a walkway between two reflecting pools. A 240-car garage at rear has direct access to lobby, arcade shops and mezzanine restaurant. The central core separates the twin towers and, with their exterior walls, provides the main vertical structural support for the building.

The over-all form of the building is uncluttered, too, both towers and central core being of the same height. The offset of the two towers from each other and from the core breaks the volume, heightens the interest and increases the access to natural light and view for the office areas—design objectives from the beginning—and allows the width of each tower to be determined by the best subdivision for perimeter offices (many were required) with a central corridor for circulation and, on some floors, for secretarial stations. The structural solution derived from this: a clear span of 42 feet, bearing wall to bearing wall in each tower. The mass of the walls at the base and the solidity of the core offer effective wind resistance.

The ceiling grid—structural beams crossed by air-conditioning ducts—is left exposed, economically providing unusual spaciousness for office area: under beams, height is 8 feet 8 inches; between beams, 11 feet. On the first and 25th floors, the 7-foot coffers thus produced are indirectly il-

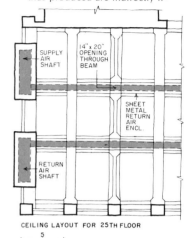

CEILING LAYOUT FOR 25TH FLOOR

luminated from fixtures edging the ducts and perimeter walls. One-fourth the usual number of fixtures results in a low-contrast, glare-free light. On the typical floors, however, a single light fixture was suspended in each coffer at a height which utilizes beams for louvering. Secretarial desks are designed to fit the storage wall (see section, bottom), and to match it. Floors are carpeted.

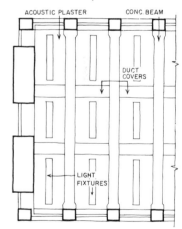

CEILING LAYOUT FOR 2ND TO 24TH FLOOR

The architects designed all company interiors and selected most of the furnishings. Interior walls are natural concrete, sandblasted, except along corridors where storage walls, finished in oak or in walnut, are used. The lobby (across page), 40 by 40 feet, appears larger because of its 15-foot windows and 21-foot ceiling, similar to ceilings throughout the building. The lighting—natural by day, indirect by night —and the felicitous handling of the reception area furnishings make this lobby exceptional for its warm and human quality and for its pleasant scale. Walls are concrete.

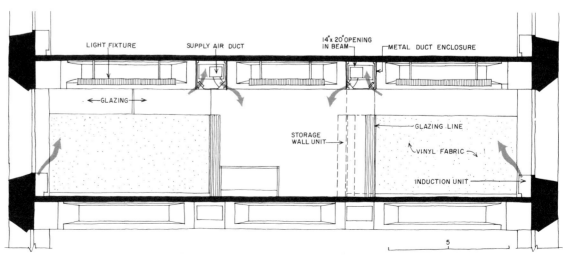

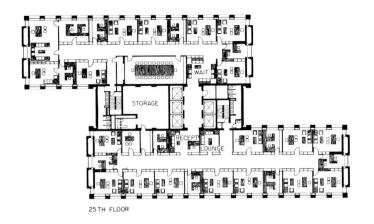

25TH FLOOR

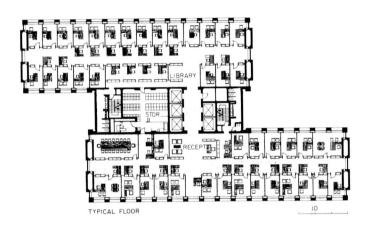

TYPICAL FLOOR

10

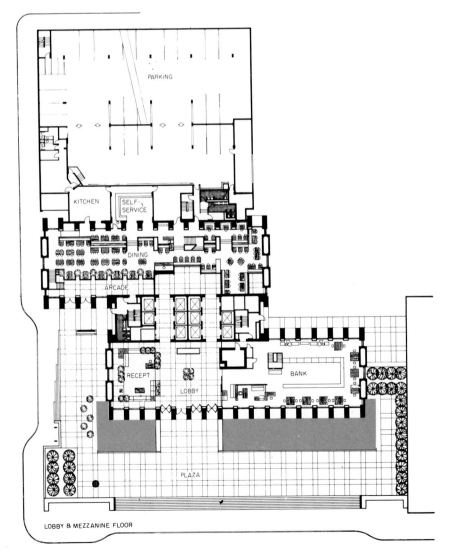

PARKING

KITCHEN

SELF-SERVICE

DINING

ARCADE

RECEPT

LOBBY

BANK

PLAZA

LOBBY & MEZZANINE FLOOR

The shopping arcade (top), originally designed as a one-story space, was altered after construction had been completed to accommodate a mezzanine floor for a restaurant and bar. Access to the arcade is from the lobby (via elevator lobby) and from the side street, across the sunken plaza. Of the small commercial areas, International Travel was designed by James Strasman of Erickson/Massey. Its area, though small, is exciting, due to the conjunction of colors (green, blue, yellow, red-brown), many lights and mirrors, which together produce the effect on the visitor of being inside a kaleidoscope.

Picadilly Place

INTERNATIONAL TRAVEL

SEATTLE-FIRST NATIONAL BANK. Seattle. Washington. Owner: Seattle-First National Bank. Architects: *Naramore, Bain, Brady & Johanson—Perry B. Johanson*, partner-in-charge; *Robert J. Pope*, project architect; *Donald A. Winkelmann*, project designer. Engineers: *Skilling, Helle, Christiansen, Robertson* (structural); *Valentine, Fisher & Tomlinson* (mechanical and electrical); consultants: *Jaros Baum Bolles* (air conditioning); *Pietro Belluschi; Carl Morse, Inc.* (construction); landscape architect: *William Teufel*; contractor: *Howard S. Wright Construction Company.*

Seattle's first very tall office building, the Seattle First National Building, looms large on the city's skyline today—but it was not designed to dominate the city. Its ultimate role, the architects intend, will be as an important—and still individual—element among many elements on the skyline, some undoubtedly taller and larger. Fifty stories high, the building looks down on even the Space Needle, relic of the World's Fair, and until recent adaption of the city's new building code, the only structure to break the old height barrier.

The process of its design, although not unique, was unusual. The client put together a team at the outset of the project, consisting of architects, structural engineers, mechanical and electrical engineers, and contractor (and two special consultants on tall buildings). All these professionals worked as a team in the analyses, design and construction of the building. The result—an elegantly detailed, handsome and functionally efficient building—is evidence of the value of the method.

The site is a large one, and its slope from Fourth Avenue to Third (47 feet difference in elevation) proved advantageous in handling the requirements for parking and for easy access by car or on foot to a banking floor. There are four levels below the Fourth Avenue Plaza, and an important entrance to the building on Third Avenue as well as at the Plaza level. The tower rises from the massive base.

Although zoning regulations in the site area permit a 10 to 1 floor area ratio, the building setback and its plazas—landscaped, and with fine additions of sculpture—provided bonuses which resulted in a 13.75 to 1 ratio. With all services in the central core, the 36 typical office floors are column free on all four sides. The tower has three subdivisions, determined by elevator and mechanical considerations. Mechanical floors, at floors 6, 19, 34 and 48, are 24 feet high, a dimension—required by air-conditioning equipment sizes—which permits incorporation of elevator machine rooms with no loss of rental space on office floors.

The Fourth Avenue Plaza level was designed with a look at the immediate and long-range future of the city. A bridge at this level will connect the adjacent building (for which the same firm is architect). The building also recognizes the possibility of an eventual rapid transit system along Third Avenue, and a system of elevated pedestrian walkways throughout the downtown core area.

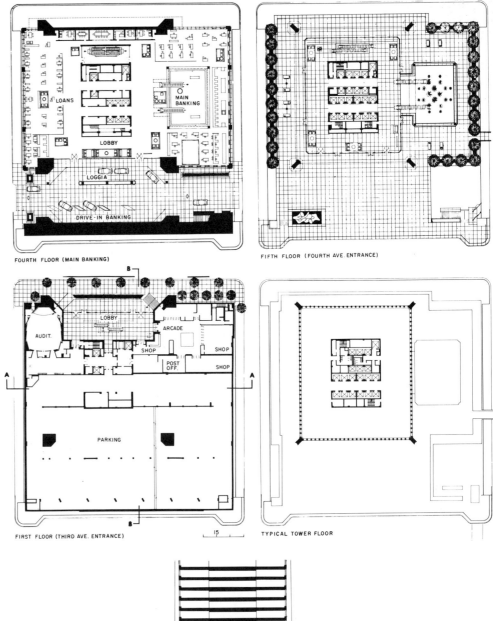

FOURTH FLOOR (MAIN BANKING)

FIFTH FLOOR (FOURTH AVE. ENTRANCE)

FIRST FLOOR (THIRD AVE. ENTRANCE)

TYPICAL TOWER FLOOR

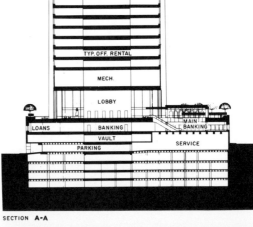

SECTION A-A

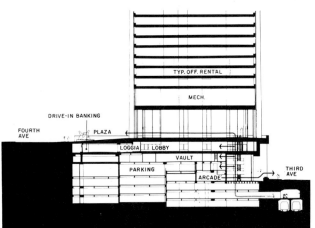

SECTION B-B

A helistop tops the building, and a restaurant is located just below that level. Executive offices for the bank occupy upper floors of the tower. There is an observation gallery as such, but on the 47th floor corner lounges, open to the rest of the floor, will provide views of the magnificent scenery on all sides.

Precision of detail is an outstanding aspect of the building. The steel skeleton of the building is repeated in the anodized aluminum cladding of each external member, and the covering for the tapered corner piers clearly expresses the elements it encloses. Other major materials used include thermal textured granite, polished granite, travertine, and bronze glass for tower glazing. Clear glass is used in the two lobbies.

The tower is a "shell wall" concept

The tower structure, based on a "shell wall" concept, is unusual: the four exterior walls actually form a very stiff box, each side of the box being designed as a vertical Vierendeel truss. Lateral wind and earthquake forces are carried down to the sixth floor level where trusses within the plane of the floor transfer these loads to the core—the core walls act as vertical plate girders. Exterior walls carry vertical load of the floors down to the sixth floor, at which point the load is transferred to the corner columns and thence to the foundation.

Each exterior wall is composed of 10 WF vertical members spaced 4 feet, 8 inches on center, and spandrels of solid steel 3 feet, 10 inches deep at typical floors. These, along with the spandrels for each floor, were fabricated in panels four stories high and two modules (4 feet, 8 inches) wide.

The columns are both architecturally and structurally significant. Clad in anodized aluminum, their outward form is designed to reflect the actual form of the enclosed steel: two plates (4 inches thick by 96 inches wide at base) separated by vertical webs (19 inches wide at base) fabricated as a box column, and located outside the building line. Between the columns at plaza level the area is dramatically kept open, the glass cage of the elevator lobby emphasizing this openness. Above the sixth floor, the columns (and the cladding) taper; at the top they are considerably smaller than at their base, as the detail (right) shows. Structurally, they continue as box columns to the 35th floor, from which point on they are normal 14 WF sections.

The aluminum cladding serves to enclose a space around the structural column which acts as a plenum, an unusual function—but exceptional conditions required an unusual solution. These columns are air conditioned with tempered air supplied at the four mechanical floors, which is circulated the length of the column to keep them at the same temperature as the core columns. This solution, plus insulation of the inside skin of the exterior walls, prevents expansion and contraction which could otherwise cause as much as a two-inch dif-

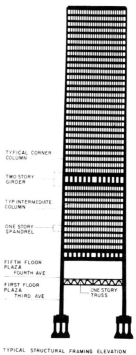

TYPICAL CORNER COLUMN

TWO STORY GIRDER

TYP INTERMEDIATE COLUMN

ONE STORY SPANDREL

FIFTH FLOOR PLAZA
FOURTH AVE

FIRST FLOOR PLAZA
THIRD AVE

ONE STORY TRUSS

TYPICAL STRUCTURAL FRAMING ELEVATION
30

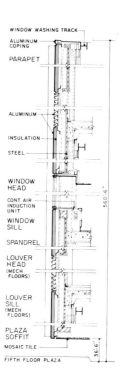

WINDOW WASHING TRACK
ALUMINUM COPING
PARAPET

ALUMINUM

INSULATION

STEEL

WINDOW HEAD

CONT. AIR INDUCTION UNIT

WINDOW SILL

SPANDREL

LOUVER HEAD (MECH FLOORS)

LOUVER SILL (MECH FLOORS)

PLAZA SOFFIT

MOSAIC TILE

FIFTH FLOOR PLAZA

560'-6"

36'-6"

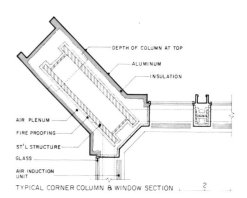

DEPTH OF COLUMN AT TOP

ALUMINUM

INSULATION

AIR PLENUM

FIRE PROOFING

ST'L STRUCTURE

GLASS

AIR INDUCTION UNIT

TYPICAL CORNER COLUMN & WINDOW SECTION
2

ference in length between exterior and core columns. Core columns, made up of 14 WF members, carry vertical loads only. All services are located in the core, freeing floor areas.

The tower rises from a 240-foot square reinforced concrete base, four levels high on one side, which acts as a long retaining wall for the soil load on the opposite side. In the base are three levels of parking, a vault floor for the bank, main banking lobby and service levels.

A favorable electricity rate (7 mils per kilowatt hour) made electric heating the most economical system. The building is the largest in the West to be so heated.

The interiors form setting for modern art

Interiors throughout the building, from the lobby on the lower level to the bank's executive offices in the tower, are enhanced by the remarkable collection of modern and contemporary art which the bank owns. Most of the 200 works of art were selected by a committee on which two of the architects, Perry Johanson and Donald Winkelmann, served. Some other works, like the mosaic on the terrace on the Third Avenue side, the Bertoia hanging wire sculpture in the main banking room, and carved benches and fountain on the plaza, were commissioned. Antoine Bourdelle's "Penelope" stands at the end of the lobby on the south side; a Jacob Epstein head is on the executive floor. The openness of the floor spaces lets everyone enjoy the displays.

The banking offices, designed by the building's architects, are handsome, inviting and unusual spaces. The main space, reached by escalator from the Plaza lobby, is below grade, but because of its location outside the building line, windows at grade on three sides make it visible from the plaza and admit daylight to the room. The drive-in offices on the same level are glass-enclosed along one side and open to view from the driveway. Warm earth colors are used both in offices and in the conference rooms along the connecting corridor.

Office space on executive floors (and on some rental floors) for which Morganelli-Heumann were architects is, for the most part, completely open and partitionless, with all desks—even those of some vice presidents—in the same space. For more private transactions, however, a bank of conference rooms against the building core is available for bank officers. This arrangement, and the open lounges opposite elevator lobbies, make the superb view of Puget Sound, and the mountains to east and west, a part of everyone's experience. A few private offices are provided.

The only shops in the building are in the arcade off the Third Avenue lobby where they are easily accessible. Naramore, Bain, Brady & Johanson designed all of them, each with its own character. Entrance to the drug store, shown here, is by a "flow-through" wall of glass panels in chrome frames which pivot at the center.

Hedrich-Blessing photos

OFFICE BUILDING FOR BLUE CROSS-BLUE SHIELD, INC. HOSPITAL SERVICE CORPORATION, Chicago. Architects and Engineers: *C. F. Murphy Associates—Otto Stark,* designer; *William Wuerfel,* project manager; contractors: *Paschen Contractors.*

Designed by C. F. Murphy Associates, this new 15-story building on North Dearborn Street at Wacker Drive is the administrative center for Blue Cross and Blue Shield in Chicago. It is a muscular, positive architectural statement on a site crowded by parking lots and a river, within a rather chaotic mixture of high-rise residences, light industry, and commercial stores. Concrete is both its frame and its exterior finish, so that the building's major structural material is also its primary design element. The eight large vertical concrete shafts combine with the eight smaller concrete columns near them to act as structural members; shafts are also duct enclosures for the heating and air conditioning. Columns and shafts carry the eye skyward, counter-balancing the strong horizontal emphasis of the concrete spandrels and cornices. The perpendicular surfaces have directional and rhythmic bush-hammered corrugations, while the horizontal surfaces are smooth, with the tie-holes exposed. The concrete ceiling of the ground floor public service area (above) continues the strength of the building inside. The brick and teak of the counter and the teak of the seating units—room for some 40 people—maintain the unity and harmony of the space.

The spacious lobby (above) is enclosed by clear glass walls set back 12½ feet from the sidewalk. The burnt-faced brick floor extends five feet beyond the exterior walls, establishing continuity with the exterior perimeter. From the south side of the lobby a bold concrete stairway (opposite page) leads directly to the employe cafeteria on the second floor. As the photos indicate, the core of the building at the lobby level is exposed, bush-hammered concrete with solid teak planking in the elevator corridors.

The lobby sculpture above was designed for the building by Louise Nevelson.

The employes' lounge (left) on the third floor is a warm, bright area with comfortable leather seating units, red cube tables, game tables and gay prints on the walls. Here again, teak was incorporated into the design of the furniture. In this space and throughout the building, air supply is integrated with the recessed air handling light troffers.

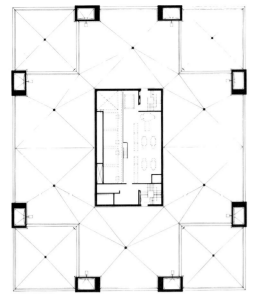

Roof plan

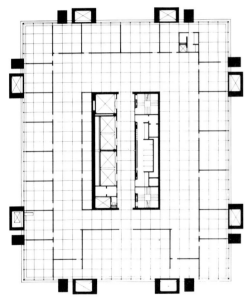

Typical office floor

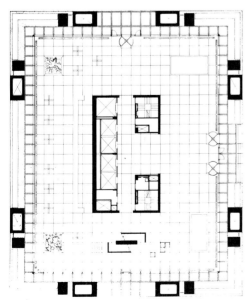

Ground floor lobby

Typical floor plans (left), the section (right) and the lobby photos indicate that the floor area surrounding the central service core is column-free. Planned on a five-foot module with movable partitions which may be elevated in any line of the grid, the design exhibits consideration for maximum efficiency and flexibility throughout the structure. In the HVAC shafts are high-velocity air supply ducts which serve a four-pipe induction system which provides cooling, heating and ventilation to the perimeter of the building. The shafts also contain the main exhaust-recirculation ducts for the entire building, domestic hot and cold water and waste and vent risers for wet stacks.

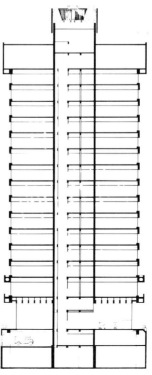

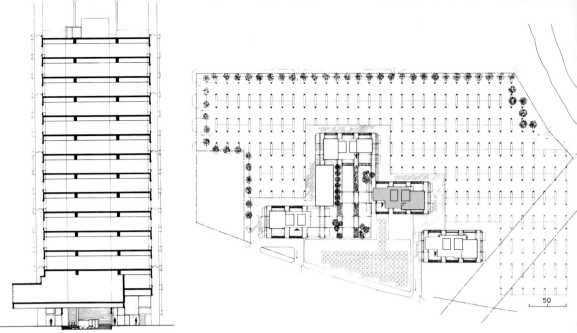

BROOKHOLLOW PLAZA, Dallas, Texas. Owner: *Brook Hollow Properties, Inc.* Associated architects: *Paul Rudolph* and *Harwood K. Smith and Partners;* structural engineering consultant: *Sepp Firnkas;* structural engineering advisor: *T.Y. Lin & Associates-Dallas;* mechanical and electrical engineers: *Herman Blum Consulting Engineers;* general contractor: *Hayman-Bryant-Andres.*

Except for the floors within the core this 130,000 square foot high rise structure is totally precast—columns, spandrels, floor-planks and core walls. The structure and the exterior exposed aggregate finishes are integral. On the interior, however, the structure is completely revealed only in the lobbies. On all other floors there are hung ceilings. The windows are mirrored glass.

As can be seen in the typical floor plan (above right) the building has a two-part core with a double stair case, elevators, lavatories and service space. The plan has been drawn in the right hand portion to indicate the linear system of construction and in the left hand portion to show the ceiling lighting grid. The floors are column free. Sixteen corners occur at every typical floor instead of the usual four, providing four times as many "corner offices," a definite advantage for a speculative office building.

When complete, the complex will consist of four high rise buildings and a two-story element containing shops and stores. Unfortunately, as the site plan indicates, the budget did not permit the construction of underground parking and the buildings will be surrounded by a sea of cars. A second tower, almost identical to the first will soon be under construction.

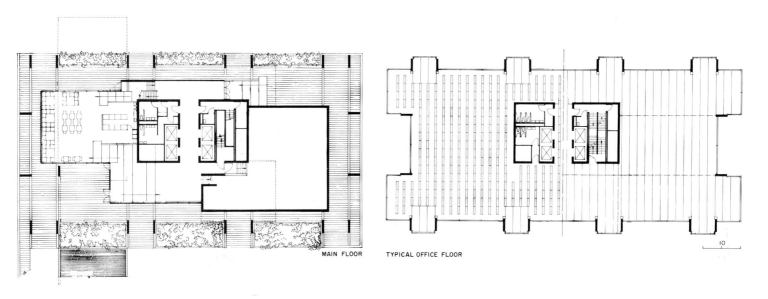

MAIN FLOOR   TYPICAL OFFICE FLOOR

10

Yukio Futagawa photos

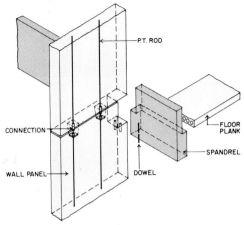

P.T. ROD

CONNECTION

WALL PANEL

DOWEL

FLOOR PLANK

SPANDREL

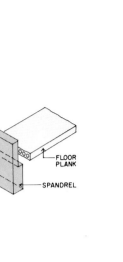

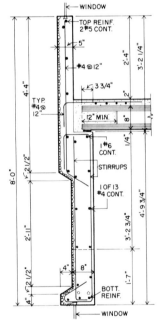

WINDOW

TOP REINF. 2#5 CONT.

5"

#4 @ 12"

3 3/4"

2"

TYP. #4 @ 12"

12" MIN.

8"

1 #6 CONT.

STIRRUPS

1 OF 13 #4 CONT.

4"

8"

BOTT. REINF.

WINDOW

2'-4"

3'-2 1/4"

4'-4"

8'-0"

2'-2 1/2"

2'-11"

2'-2 1/2"

4"

1/4"

4'-9 3/4"

3'-2 3/4"

1'-7"

SPANDREL - FLOOR SLAB CONNECTION

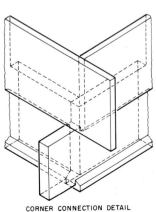

CORNER CONNECTION DETAIL

Brookhollow Plaza's owning company is a subsidiary of Texas Industries, Inc. who produce among other products, cement, concrete block and ready mix. TXI was subcontractor for the casting and erection of all the precast components. The basic structural design was developed by consulting engineer Sepp Firnkas based upon the modular wall and floor system he has developed for housing (top detail). On the Brookhollow project his bearing walls have become 8-ft-high column supported spandrels as shown in the detail drawing at left and in the photos.

There are 20 post-tensioned exterior columns 6 ft wide by 1 ft thick on the building's long dimensions and 7 ft by 1 ft at the ends. At one of the corners (top photo) the columns have been engineered to extend 43 ft without bracing. Rudolph's precast joint (detail below) is not only handsome, but it represents an advance over the usual butted or mitered precast connections which require extremely fine tolerances. "In this design I have celebrated the joints" explains Rudolph.

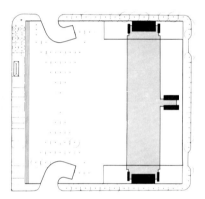

FEDERAL RESERVE BANK OF MINNEAPOLIS. Architects: *Gunnar Birkerts and Associates—project director: Charles Fleckenstein; director of production: Vytautas Usas; director of field administration: Gunars Ejups; interiors: Barbara J. Bos.* Engineers: *Skilling, Helle, Christiansen, Robertson* (structural); *Shannon & Wilson, Inc.* (foundation); *Jaros, Baum & Bolles* (mechanical /electrical). Consultants: *Cerami and Associates, Inc.* (mechanical/electrical); *Geiger & Hamme, Inc.* (acoustical); *McKee-Berger-Mansueto, Inc.* (cost); *Arthur W. Dana & Associates* (food operations); *Hubert Wilke, Inc.* (audio-visual). Landscape architects: *Charles Wood & Associates, Inc.* General contractor: *Knutson Construction Company.* Plaza Sculpture: *Charles Perry, Dmitri Hadzi, and Paul Granlund.*

Photos below and overleaf courtesy of The Federal Reserve Bank of Minneapolis

Balthazar Korab photos

The new Federal Reserve Bank of Minneapolis is by just about any standards an impressive realization of impressive aims, even if some of those aims are discredited or discounted or misunderstood by some architects. But there it is—big, bold and real, the product of the enthusiasm and imagination of the client, the architects and the engineers. As such it is a building to be reckoned with.

The architects have taken a complicated program and rendered it in clear and unforgettable terms. Security operations which require protected facilities (about 60 per cent of the total square footage) are below the ground underneath a sloping plaza. Clerical and administrative operations are housed in an office block suspended from two great concrete towers. The catenary members which support the office floors are echoed in the curtain wall. Below the curve the glass stands forward; above it stands behind. For clean and strong architectural gesture, the likes of this solution have not been seen very often in recent years. Ask anybody in Minneapolis about the Federal Reserve building; if they draw a blank, then describe a catenary with your hand and they'll know what you mean. That fact in itself represents an achievement of sorts.

The architects' design commanded an unusual performance by the structural engineers. Most knew that it was possible to build an office building with a column-free span of 275 feet, but until now no one had actually done it, and few would quibble over the reported price tag of $47 a square foot. In concept the structure is simple. Two catenaries, one on either side of the building and 60 feet apart, support the major facades. These are rigid frames which in turn support the concrete slab floors. The tendency of the supporting towers at either end to topple inwards is checked by two 28-foot-deep trusses at the top of the building; the space in between them contains the mechanical equipment. One result of all these labors is a set of eminently flexible work spaces. Another result is the creation of a 2.5 acre public plaza sloping gently upward to a height of 20 feet above the entrance level of the building (photo, page 157).

The original Federal Reserve Bank of Minneapolis, like many of the other banks in the system, was built in the early 20's and was a windowless, forbidding structure. Its architect, Cass Gilbert, described it as "a strongbox for the currency of the Northwest." The president of the Bank today echoes Gilbert's concern for security, but he also adds a new twist: "The responsibility of the Bank to serve the financial community and the public requires openness and accessibility." This without question is an admirable intention, resulting in offices with a view, and a plaza for the general public.

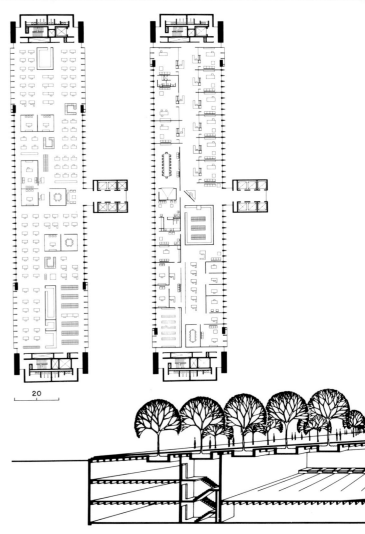

20

Typical floors of the above-ground portion of the bank are organized in an open plan, with certain areas where privacy is desired screened off by movable partitions, one of which can be seen in the photograph above right. The executive offices have fixed walls (photo above). The lobby of the building is shown at right.

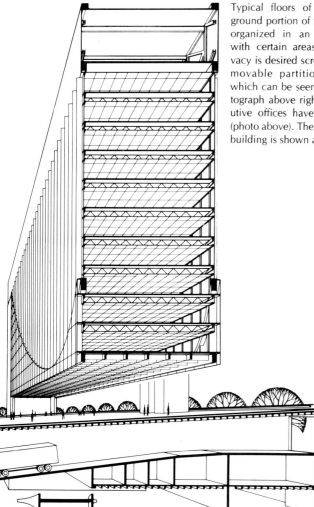

THE CLEVELAND TRUST COMPANY HEAD-
QUARTERS, Cleveland, Ohio. Architects: *Marcel
Breuer and Hamilton Smith;* associated architects for
local supervision: *Flynn, Dalton, Van Dijk & Partners.*
Engineers: *Weidlinger Associates* (structural); *Barber
& Hoffman* (soil), *H. W. H. Associates* (mechanical/
electrical); Consultants: *Lewis S. Goodfriend and Associates* (acoustical); *David Mintz Lighting Associates*
(lighting); *Frazier, Orr, Fairbank & Quam Inc.* (interior
design); *Sandgren and Murtha, Inc.* (graphics); *Raymond C. Daly* (general construction); *Norwell Bur-
gess* (bank operations). General contractor: *Turner
Construction Company.*

The new Cleveland Trust Company pre-
serves an important city landmark while at the
same time it reinforces and invigorates its urban
setting. The decision to preserve the original
banking building erected in 1907 meant the
permanent dedication to the city of the air space
above this structure. Only the first stage of the
tower has been built so far. The future wing can
be seen in the plans (opposite page, bottom).
The tower's 1,314 precast concrete panels of
grey Vermont granite aggregate form a non-ab-
sorptive surface which discourages the accu-
mulation of soot and dirt. As the details (below)
indicate, the inside corners have been rounded
so as to eliminate dirt-catching crevices. This
self-cleaning design includes channels for rainwater chased into the outside edges of the
panels. By means of this device, rainwater never
drains across more than one panel, thus eliminating staining. The building will weather more
evenly, from top to bottom.

Erol Akyavas photos

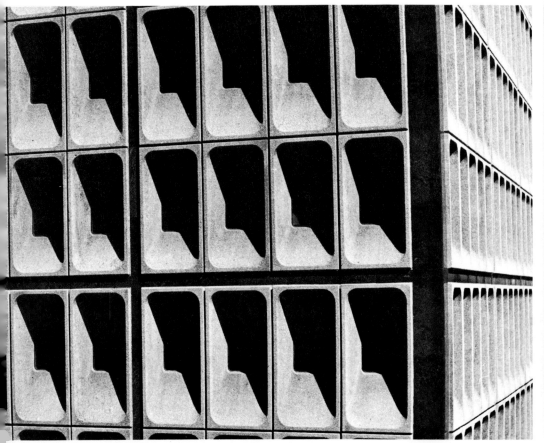

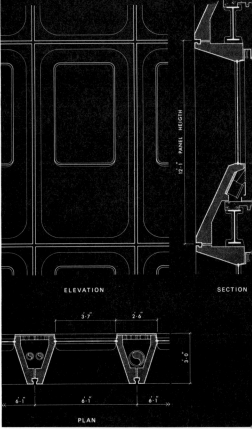

ELEVATION   SECTION

PLAN

162

1 Entrance lobby
2 Connection to existing corner bank
3 Banking lobby
4 Clerical
5 Storage
6 Truck dock
7 Receiving

8 Existing corner bank
9 Second-phase construction
10 Meeting room foyer
11 Meeting room
12 Infirmary
13 Balcony connection
14 Office space

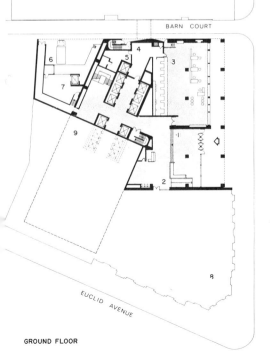

GROUND FLOOR

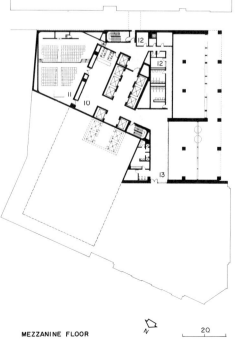

MEZZANINE FLOOR

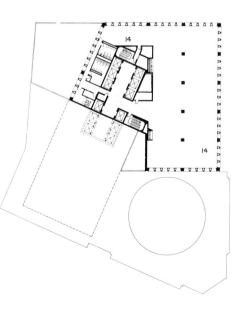

TYPICAL FLOOR

163

The 41 caissons drilled for this steel-framed structure are the deepest ever sunk for a commercial building. Extending over 200 feet to bedrock, they provide the most solid possible foundation to rigidly limit the differentials between the tower and the surrounding buildings to which it connects. The core—containing the elevators, fire stairs and chases for mechanical and electrical equipment—was constructed by the slip-forming process. The core rose at the rate of one floor per work day. The precast wall panels contain cavities molded into their inside faces which conceal the structural framing as well as heating and air conditioning equipment. The elimination thereby of projecting heating units and columns adds immeasurably to the efficiency of perimeter working areas.

Granite contrasts with the precast concrete in the main floor lobby and public spaces. The highly polished black stone is used to clad windowless wall surfaces and to form subdivisions of the bank front under the ground floor colonnade (below left). Granite is also used in its rough "fire-polished" state. Lobby walls are finished in granite tile, elevator doors are framed with granite plinths, and the bank tellers' desks are ranged behind a parapet and counter of this durable and elegant stone.

This extensive use of masonry materials of quality, weight, durability and permanence, which at the same time provide deeply molded surfaces, is in harmony with the architectural character of the landmark which the new tower adjoins.

HIGH-RISE
TECHNOLOGY

As office buildings become taller and less heavy, while at the same time their structural systems are more clearly articulated, they present many new challenges to those who must design and detail them. In the interest of this structural clarity, the skeleton framework of these skyscrapers is often placed on the exterior, and the exposed members must thus be insulated to offset expansion and contraction brought about by temperature changes. Even moderate thermal changes cause structural and partitioning problems. The first article in this section discusses the temperature criteria for the outside structural members of the John Hancock building in Chicago (pages 168–170) and describes the method of thermal insulation.

The two-part article "Solving Today's Curtain Wall Problems" (pages 171–178) points out that, in spite of the technological advances of the past decade, many curtain walls still leak, glass panes break or blow out, and spandrels and sashes stain. Some proposed remedies include a general upgrading of standards.

Since buildings have shed their heavy masonry skins, wind loads have become a problem. Simple post-and-beam rigid frames become inefficient above 20 stories because of wind. New families of structural systems have evolved, each suitable for given ranges of heights, in steel, concrete or their combination, and these are described in the third article, "Optimizing the Structure of the Skyscraper." The last article on the 54-story One Liberty Plaza building in New York City sets forth its advances in rigid-frame design and new approaches to the fire protection of the exterior steel framing.

Insulated aluminum covers sheathe John Hancock building

The unique, tapered steel box that forms the structure of the 100-story John Hancock Center in Chicago had to be clothed in an insulated skin to prevent movement that otherwise would result when outdoor temperature rises and falls. Temperature change was a factor because the structural frame, with its diagonals which take both vertical and wind loads, is expressed as part of the architectural esthetic, putting the frame out in the open.

Aluminum skin is a principal feature of the exterior of the building, outlining the main structural members that trace a striking design on the faces of the building. If these "exposed" members had been left uninsulated, temperature variations would have caused the steel frame to expand or contract. Compensation may be effected by providing expansion jointing—but when a structure rises about 50 stories, such jointing may greatly increase the cost and reduce the efficiency of the building.

After the basic architectural design of the building had been worked out, architects Skidmore, Owings & Merrill were faced with the need for an integrally insulated cladding material that would satisfy simultaneously the engineering requirements of the structure and the esthetic values desired. The engineering requirement was to maintain beam-center temperature of the steel at 69 ± 1F under an 87 F differential. Materials evaluation included consideration of aluminum, steel, limestone, brick and precast concrete. Weight factors associated with a building of this height immediately eliminated all materials except aluminum and steel considering such factors as durability; ease of fabrication, erection and maintenance; esthetic contribution; and cost.

All aluminum finishes were considered, including natural processed and painted aluminum and various anodized finishes. They were evaluated on the basis of published performance specifications and upon their esthetic compatability with the structure and its environment. Weatherability, uniformity and resistance to flaking and chipping were the principal criteria. A high-density anodized finish was selected. Black was chosen for the column cover cladding, bronze for the window framing. Colors ranging from light bronze through black were evaluated.

The insulating capability of the column cladding is of vital importance to the functioning of the building, since even moderate temperature changes in the exterior columns can create serious structural and partition problems. The unit is designed so that the center of the vertical and diagonal steel beams are maintained at a temperature of 69 ± 1F when a temperature differential of 87 F (from −13 F to 74 F) exists across

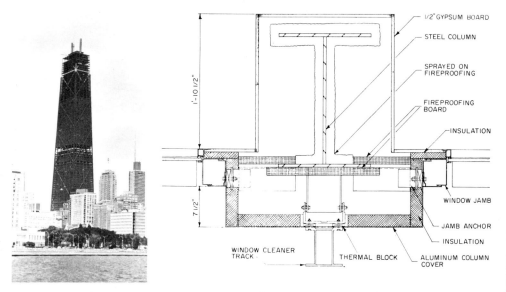

1/2" GYPSUM BOARD

STEEL COLUMN

SPRAYED ON FIREPROOFING

FIREPROOFING BOARD

INSULATION

WINDOW JAMB

JAMB ANCHOR

INSULATION

ALUMINUM COLUMN COVER

WINDOW CLEANER TRACK

THERMAL BLOCK

1'-10 1/2"

7 1/2"

168

Steel skeleton of the 100-story-high John Hancock building in Chicago is clad in gray anodized aluminum. A critical function of the column covers was to maintain temperature of the structural members at 69 ± 1 F to avoid problems that would result from expansion and contraction caused by change in the outdoor temperature. For this reason, the vertical, diagonal and major horizontal covers were insulated with 2 in. of urethane insulation. The corner columns were, however, insulated with 4 in. of urethane because of the greater exposure and size of these columns. The steel frame is fire-protected by sprayed-on asbestos material.

To demonstrate that the insulated cladding could maintain proper temperature, a column mock-up was made with the exterior side sealed in a chamber that could be cooled to produce an 87 F differential. Thermocouples were installed on the cladding unit and the column.

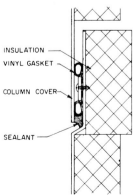

INSULATION
VINYL GASKET

COLUMN COVER

SEALANT

COLUMN COVER SPLICE

an external face and internal wall of the building. Because temperature control is so important, the cladding suppliers successfully carried out prolonged and extensive testing of the cladding's insulating capabilities with full-scale mock-ups to prove the design's ability to maintain specified limits.

The cladding units vary in size depending on their location in the building. The vertical column covers at the base of the building are 4 ft-6 in. wide and 18 in. deep. At the top of the building (the 100th floor) they are 2 ft-6 in. wide and 5½-in. deep. All the column units are built in one-story lengths, which vary depending on the floor-to-floor height. The typical office floors from the 4th floor through the 36th floor are 12 ft-6 in. Apartment floors are an average of 9 ft-3 in. There are actually three different floor-to-floor dimensions within the apartment area with the group from the 46th through the 54th floor being 9 ft-6 in., the 57th floor through the 73rd floor being 9 ft-3 in., and the 76th floor through the 90th floor being 9 ft-0 in. The other floor heights varied depending upon their use and location within the building. The longest column covers were used on the 44th floor, which is the sky lobby. These are 15 ft-10 in. long. The column covers from the 2nd floor to the 21st floor were made from 3/16-in.-thick sheet aluminum. The column covers for the 5th floor, complete with insulation, closure extrusions and window cleaner track, weighed approximately 430 pounds. A single column cover at the 98th floor, being made of ⅛-in. sheet of a smaller size but including the same window cleaner track and closure extrusions, weighed 215 pounds.

There are approximately 4,200 cladding units. This includes all covers for the vertical columns, diagonal columns and major horizontal covers occurring at the 2nd, 21st, 38th, 56th, 75th, 92nd and 100th floors. These horizontal covers differ from the vertical and diagonal column covers only by modifications of the side extrusions.

The aluminum sheets were brake-formed into the channel shape cover using a 16-ft long brake press. At the upper end of each of the covers the sheet material was offset 9/16-in. to provide an overlapping joint into the cover above. This joint was designed to include a double-sealing tubular vinyl extrusion and a primary sealant. Extruded adaptors are attached with conventional threaded connectors on each side of the column cover to accept the window and spandrel units. This extrusion incorporates provision for a double line of sealant between the extrusion and the column cover itself. (See description of temperature and weather-proof testing.)

On the face of each vertical column cover is a large window cleaner track extrusion. This extrusion was attached after the anodic finish was applied to both the track and the column cover. The vertical, diagonal and horizontal covers were insulated with 2-in. thick urethane foam. The corner columns, due to the greater exposure and larger size, were insulated with 4-in. urethane. All of the insulation material was attached to the vertical column covers with aluminum insulation nails, applied with a stud welder.

Test procedures for wind and rain resistance

The wall system was fully tested to assure rain and wind resistance. Earlier, however, a 1/300 scale aluminum model of the John Hancock Center, as well as models of all buildings within a 1000-ft radius of the center, were wind-tunnel tested to ascertain drag and gust coefficients and static wind pressures on the surface of the building at different heights, and with the simulated wind coming from any direction. There were pressure orifices at a number of points on all faces of the model to detect both positive and negative pressures. Static wind pressure from all directions was found to be affected significantly by the turbulence caused by the surrounding buildings, and as a result pressures were considerably

lower than had been calculated for unhindered flow.

In order to produce wind velocities up to 135 mph and to simulate the effects of a rain storm more severe than Chicago is ever likely to experience, a World War II Navy Corsair fighter plane—minus its tail and most of its wings but retaining its 2100 hp engine driving—was used to simulate the wind. For the test, a replica of a section of the aluminum and glass curtain wall was used. Engine speed was increased until a wind of approximately 100 mph blew steadily on the curtain wall assembly. At this point, jets of water located in front of the assembly were turned on, creating the rain-storm effect. The throttle was advanced to produce wind gusts with a velocity up to 135 mph for 10 minutes.

The inner surface of the curtain wall was kept under observation under spotlights to assure that there were no leaks during the rain-storm test. It is not anticipated that the panel would ever have to withstand these conditions in actual service.

In order to simulate wind loading of another sort, the test chamber behind the curtain wall assembly is equipped with a vacuum pump, permitting partial evacuation of the chamber. In another test, the chamber was pressurized, making the curtain wall flex outwards as it would under the suction created by winds parallel to the building surface, or in the lee. In these tests, wall deflection was measured by dial gauges.

To demonstrate that the aluminum insulated cladding could maintain beam center temperature at 69 ±1 F, a column mock-up was prepared with the exterior side of the column sealed in a chamber, which could be cooled so as to produce the 87 F temperature differential. Thermocouples were attached at various points of the cladding unit assembled to a column sample to monitor temperature of the outer and interior surfaces and primarily of the steel column. The column assembly tested was 5-ft high by 2 ft, 10-in. wide and measured 3-ft in depth.

A mocked-up section of wall was tested for its integrity against wind-driven rain and for deflection resulting from wind speeds as high as 135 mph. The wind was produced by the engine from a World War II Navy Corsair. After the engine was producing a 100 mph wind, water jets were turned on to create the rainstorm effect. The test chamber behind the curtain wall assembly can be partially evacuated by a vacuum pump; or, on the other hand, it can be pressurized. The latter test demonstrates the effect of suction forces on the glass created by winds parallel to the surface, or on the leeward side of the building. Dial gauges were used to measure the deflection.

Solving today's curtain wall problems: comprehending them, and then providing expert attention

Technologically, the modern curtain wall has come a long way in 20 years. At the time the UN Secretariat and Lever House were built, a break was made from relatively simple window technology to curtain wall systems which have grown ever more sophisticated, and with which problems are significantly different. The behavior of curtain walls in warding off the effects of the weather is highly complex. They may look simple, but are far from it. Rather, they are involved assemblies of structure, metal and glass working, with much interrelationship and interdependence of elements. Further, there is much to know about finishes, and many subtle things to know about sealants. Yet, the know-how for the design and construction of curtain walls that will have a minimum of problems exists today.

Unfortunately, however, problems with curtain walls have not disappeared. Though some of the manifestations of problems— leakage, broken glass—remain the same as in the early days, the reasons for them are quite different. Twenty years ago little was known about the physical behavior of curtain walls; glazing gaskets were being used for the first time, and new high-performance sealants were introduced only after the putty type failed to work in new situations. Since that time vast knowledge has accumulated, and many new effective materials have been made available.

Curtain walls and the building process are more complex—so are the problems

So, why failures today? Mainly, the reasons are these:

1. The curtain wall has not been comprehended by designers as a system. For example, the deformation of a wall under wind loading may not be deleterious structurally, but on the other hand, this movement could open the glazing system to water penetration.

An architect might assume that any wall configuration should be possible. While this might be so strictly from a fabrication standpoint, it is not realistic with respect to resistance to water penetration. Some wall shapes literally invite the rain to come in. Thus there is a technical discipline —not just to be reckoned with, but perhaps even exploited in terms of design expression.

2. The realities of field tolerances and thermal expansion and contraction have not been taken fully into account. Columns

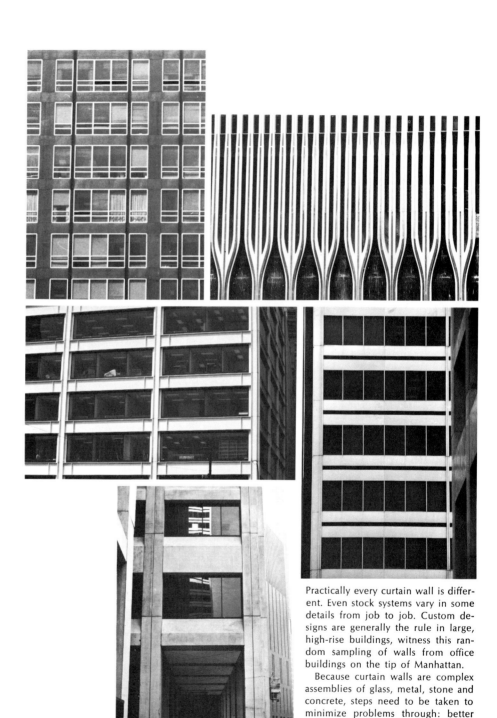

Practically every curtain wall is different. Even stock systems vary in some details from job to job. Custom designs are generally the rule in large, high-rise buildings, witness this random sampling of walls from office buildings on the tip of Manhattan.

Because curtain walls are complex assemblies of glass, metal, stone and concrete, steps need to be taken to minimize problems through: better understanding of the curtain wall as a system, appreciation of the influences of the market place, and recognition of field problems that affect design and specifications.

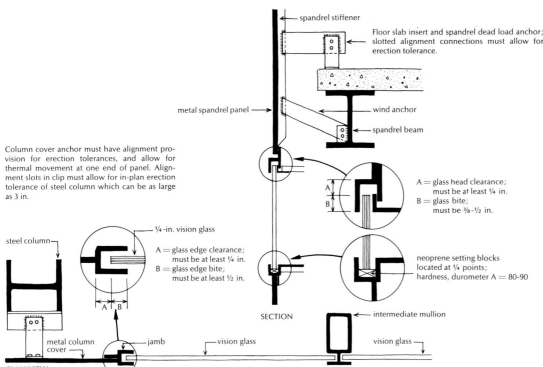

spandrel stiffener

Floor slab insert and spandrel dead load anchor; slotted alignment connections must allow for erection tolerance.

metal spandrel panel

wind anchor

spandrel beam

A = glass head clearance; must be at least ¼ in.
B = glass bite; must be ⅜-½ in.

metal column cover

neoprene setting blocks located at ¼ points; hardness, durometer A = 80-90

intermediate mullion

SECTION

Column cover anchor must have alignment provision for erection tolerances, and allow for thermal movement at one end of panel. Alignment slots in clip must allow for in-plan erection tolerance of steel column which can be as large as 3 in.

¼-in. vision glass

A = glass edge clearance; must be at least ¼ in.
B = glass edge bite; must be at least ½ in.

steel column

metal column cover — jamb — vision glass — vision glass

PLAN VIEW

note: curtain wall components are at a larger scale for clarity

Not accounting for building tolerances can lead to trouble—for the wall, and for the glass.

It tolerances are not properly considered in the design of curtain wall anchorages, it may be difficult for the erectors to get glass openings plumb and square. When this happens, glaziers are tempted to trim the glass on site which reduces its strength, particularly with respect to thermal loading. Further, erectors may find it difficult to align the curtain wall components.

An example of a tolerance condition is this: it is accepted practice to permit steel columns to be off the building line as much as 2 in. out and 1 in. in with respect to the core; therefore, the column cover anchor must allow for this, and the floor slab insert and spandrel anchor must accommodate both spandrel beam deflection and column tolerances.

---

can be out of line by several inches; spandrel beams will have a certain deflection that may or may not be what was anticipated; glass, as cut, may vary slightly from the dimensioned size.

3. Structurally, curtain walls are being designed closer and closer to the loads they have to withstand in the field. In the early days, curtain walls were considerably overdesigned. Manufacturers, themselves, tended to be conservative because of inexperience in the engineering and fabrication of modern curtain walls. But by now they have a much broader experience. The main reason, however, for manufacturers designing and fabricating curtain walls closer and closer to minimum required strengths is that the market place has become much more competitive. Further, their factory and erection labor costs are much higher. So, walls are no longer conservatively designed; and there is less and less room for error in design load assumptions, for accommodating construction deficiencies, and for coping with unforeseen contingencies (such as the construction of a new building nearby that changes the wind load pattern).

4. The rush of owners to get buildings enclosed, occupied, and producing income may force subcontractors into poor construction practices. Because glazing openings may turn out to be neither plumb nor square, glaziers may resort to nipping corners and seaming edges in order to get the glass to fit, and in the process weakening the glass. The owner may accept, to his later chagrin, improperly erected sections of curtain wall rather than slow down construction.

As mentioned earlier, the two most

common failures associated with curtain walls are leakage and glass breakage, with the former being by far the more prevalent. Of course there can be other problems that have no potential physical harm to property or people, but may be disturbing psychologically — e.g., creaking and popping noises caused by movement of the curtain wall against the building frame; vibration of large panes of glass caused by wind; defects in the appearance of the curtain wall such as staining, lack of color match, oil-canning, show-through from the back of panel reinforcement, etc.

Glass failures can be dramatic, but are patently avoidable when care is taken

Aside from accidents, glass breakage occurs when it is overloaded by wind, or, in the case of tinted glass, when it is overstressed thermally; occasionally, the two effects can be combined. Apparently, most of the glass breakage caused by the wind occurs during the construction period, or at least after the first few wind storms. Glass strength is a statistical matter, and, when practical factors of safety are used, a small amount of breakage can be expected—say 8 lights in 1000. Thus, during the early life of a building, the lights termed "weak sisters" are broken and replaced. Thereafter a building in which the glazing has been properly designed should be relatively free of trouble.

As a safety precaution, owners of high-rise buildings being built in downtown areas of large cities may have streets blocked off on very windy days, to avoid passersby being hurt.

But breakage during construction is probably more prevalent than it used to be. At least it is more noticeable. For one

thing, architects are calling for larger lights of glass and more of them. Further, it seems that the structure is hardly up when the curtain wall and its glass are installed, in part to enable other trades to work regardless of the weather. Thus it is easier for glass to be damaged by debris and through the carelessness of workmen.

(The strength of glass in resisting wind load is a function of its thickness and the polish of its surface; the glass is weakened by scratches and abrasions.)

Even undamaged glass can fail, however, if it is not properly supported. For example if the framing or gasketing that holds the glass can be excessively distorted, the glass may fail. If the gasket is too flexible because of shape, size, or insufficient hardness, a phenomenon called roll-off may occur, which may result in the entire light of glass being blown out of the gasket.

Glass breakage often is a direct result of proper erection practices not being followed, particularly with regard to handling and cutting of glass, and attentiveness in maintaining correct erection tolerances and plumbness and squareness of openings. It is often found in high-rise construction, particularly with stick-type curtain-wall systems, that tolerances for the building's structural system are greater than they should have been. Then, it turns out that glazing openings may not be plumb or square and that opening dimensions have not been maintained. The glazier's answer in order to get the glass to fit may be to trim the glass on the job which weakens it, particularly in its resistance to thermal load. And if a crack gets started in a light of glass because of thermal load, it can be more easily broken by wind.

It's the unsuspected things that cause problems with glass breakage due to wind and to thermal load

Still not sufficiently recognized is the extent of negative wind loading at the corners of buildings—as much as 2.5 times the positive load on the windward side. This fact needs to be considered in the sizing of glass. If the glass lacks the recommended amount of bite, or is installed poorly, or gets damaged during installation, it obviously is much more susceptible to breakage at the corners.

The sketch at far right is a hypothetical example by Fazlur Kahn showing glass thicknesses based upon variation of wind load with building height and the wind load coefficients for both corner and interior areas of the facade. For practical reasons the glass thickness would be constant for a given floor.

Shading of tinted glass by building projections can result in high stresses. If the edges of glass are damaged, its strength to resist these stresses is lowered.

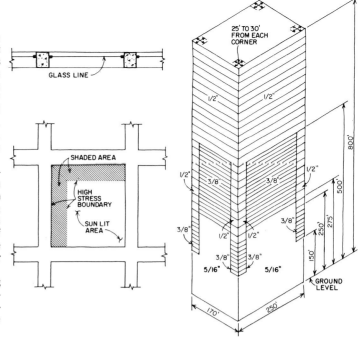

The result of proper tolerances not being maintained may be that some lights of glass do not have sufficient bite provided by the glazing pocket or gasket, perhaps only ¼ in. or so. Such lights are susceptible to wind damage.

Another common cause of breakage of glass during the construction period is that the glass lights may not be fully glazed in the beginning by the contractor. That is, the glazing system may be such that he can safely support the glass in the glazing opening, under normal conditions, without having fully installed all glazing materials—the sealant that goes in the rabbet, or the zipper that goes in the neoprene gasket. The glazing contractor might not finish the job for months. Because the glass is not tightly held, a high wind may blow out some of the glass.

When glazing openings are out-of-square, all sorts of makeshift arrangements may have to be resorted to—jacks to try to force the opening into square; torches to alter anchorages, specially cut glass to fit the openings, side-shimming of glass in an out-of-square opening to maintain proper bite on all edges.

Because of lack of control of opening dimensions, some buildings have suffered continuous glass loss for a year or more until all the glass that may have been nipped or cut on the job to make it fit was replaced.

Field problems are the most common, but occasionally the design is marginal

Obviously the proper installation of glass is a critical factor in obtaining designed-for strength. For example, glass-to-metal contact in the glazing rabbet can result in point loading that causes glass to break. To avoid this situation a clearance of around ⅛ in. should be maintained between the face of the glass and the face of the glazing stop. Face shimming is required in lights of glass over 100 united inches (i.e., total perimeter) in size. It is difficult to install intermittent shims properly so that they work, so a continuous face shim is frequently used, consisting of a relatively hard butyl tape that will not distort, or a softer tape that has a hard core.

There may be faults with the curtain wall components, themselves, that interfere with proper installation of glass. For example, it sometimes happens that welds are not ground down in glazing pockets. Occasionally a wrong component is supplied—such as a different clip than intended being used to hold a curtain wall panel to a mullion, causing glass to metal contact.

Field problems, however, are the more prevalent. A further example is that of welding spatter which can seriously damage glass if it is unprotected. The New York City building code calls for glass to be protected by a hardboard covering or its equivalent where glass may be close to welding operations or near material hoists (temporarily omitting the glass is another solution).

Sometimes field conditions combine to create difficult glazing conditions. Example: glazing opening too small; glass a little large; weather cold; glazing pocket minimal for esthetic reasons. Invariably, it seems, tolerances seem to accumulate against the installer. If glazing is done in cold weather with gaskets, and the glass is slightly large, the glazier is tempted to seam (file) the edges to avoid tearing the gasket.

Occasionally, particularly on "budget" jobs, everything can go wrong, resulting in extensive loss of glass. Design can be in error (with respect to tolerances and glazing techniques); fabrication can be faulty; installation can be poor. It is known that, under these circumstances, one owner had to replace 30 per cent or more of the glass that may have cost, after the fact, 50-60 per cent of the original cost of the wall.

Again, on "budget" jobs, the design may be so skinned down, that the wall itself is not strong enough to hold the glass. When the wind blows hard, the results may be catastrophic. A high-rise apartment building in the Midwest is known to have lost over 100 lights of glass during a winter wind storm, reportedly because the wall was not strong enough.

When sizing glass thickness, the designer must know the loads, consider the support

Once in awhile the glass that the designer selects is not thick enough for the most severe loading conditions to be encountered. Under optimum circumstance (i.e. proper bite, clearance, etc.), the glass might have been strong enough, but then, because of the way it was installed, the glass was not able to work to capacity.

On the other hand, the actual extent of the wind load on the glass in service is not always accurately predicted, particularly the negative loads created at corners of buildings which may be as high as 2.5 times the direct, positive load of the wind on the windward face of the building.

As is so with other aspects of building, occasionally there is the tendency to use values required by code (which are usually minimum) for design purposes. These values may seem reasonable enough to a designer—who says to himself that a 30 lb per sq ft load is equivalent to a 100 mph wind, and, furthermore, he is aware of buildings in the vicinity that have used this value and weathered many a storm. But maybe the building he is working on has a number of re-entrant corners; maybe the building is in an unusual environmental situation (perhaps a canyon effect with wind); maybe adjacent buildings create an unusual loading condition. He may, therefore, be taking a much bigger risk than he realizes.

Though glass is not a ductile material such as steel, nonetheless like a steel plate it has its greatest capacity under load if it is supported along four edges. A number of recent buildings have used large lights of glass with butted edges and no intermediate mullions, the joint being sealed with silicone, to give the appearance of huge, unbroken expanses of glass. Obviously glass used in this way has less capacity than if it were uniformly supported along four edges, and, consequently the glass has to be quite a bit thicker.

The other cause of glass failure, mentioned earlier, is thermally-induced breakage that occurs with tinted, solar-heat-absorbing glasses when the edges have been damaged during installation, or in service, and particularly when there are uneven stresses caused by partial shading of the lights. This kind of failure is potentially less hazardous to passersby because the cracking can be noticed by building occupants or maintenance personnel, whereas glass failures caused by wind can come without warning.

Obviously, the more heat absorbent the glass, the higher the stress induced by the heat of the sun. Light-reflective glasses are loaded even more severely than the tinted heat-absorbing glasses because the reflective coating is on the air-space side of the inner light of a double-glazed unit. Thus, because more heat is trapped due to the "greenhouse effect," such glass can get hotter than ordinary tinted glass. Special consideration should be given to this problem with very large lights of glass.

The wind produces capricious effects on buildings, but they are predictable

Most glass and curtain-wall failures caused by wind have occurred in tall high-rise buildings. But engineers have the design tools to properly design glass; not perfectly, but satisfactorily—according to Leslie E. Robertson, partner in the consulting engineering firm of Skilling, Helle, Christiansen, Robertson, structural engineers for the World Trade Center and for the U.S. Steel Building. Analysis and design can be done for a building that can provide the same level of strength for all lights of glass, rather than having some strong and some excessively weak. Predictions of breakage rates will be reasonable. Technology does not preclude a reasonable design, says Robert-

son; validity is sufficiently high.

With buildings of unusual configuration, or buildings that are particularly large, Robertson feels that wind tunnel testing may be advisable. For a few thousand dollars, he says, a wind tunnel test can be performed from which wind loads can be predicted. The engineer can develop a good glass design with respect to strength that is rational and that seems to work. The cost of the wind tunnel testing and the resultant design of the glass may represent a cost savings or a cost increase from design by experience; in any case, according to Robertson, neither would be significant in terms of total building cost.

Obviously some discretion has to be exercised as to when wind-tunnel testing should be used. With many tall buildings that are not out of the ordinary, the range of pressures that can be expected are pretty well understood. An engineer can look at what has been done on other structures and have a reasonable understanding of what to expect, particularly when there are no remarkable differences between buildings. The designer must remember, however, that wind speeds in Florida are going to be higher than those in Los Angeles, and that wind load pressures are velocity-dependent to the second power. If you put the same glass design in both locations, you will have a problem.

An interesting phenomenon of wind with respect to glass breakage is that this is only partly associated with steady-state pressures. Actually, there are rapid fluctuations in pressure which are associated with the separation of flow of wind from the face of the building and reattachment of the wind to the face; the reattachment line fluctuates rapidly back and forth depending upon the angle of attack of the wind and the building configuration—corners, indentations in the facade, etc. Glass breakage seems to be associated more with fluctuating pressure than steady state pressure. Though glass behaves stronger the faster it is loaded, the fact that pressures are velocity-sensitive to the second power, means that a small increase in velocity produces a big increase in pressure.

Historically, the glass breakage problem has been recognized and considered in the design process. The same is true for leakage—there is a lot of expertise on how to keep out water, and many solutions are incredibly ingenious. What is not really known, however is how the large number of curtain walls erected in the last 10 years will behave under the catastrophic loading of the eastern seaboard's hurricane winds. For large, special buildings, mock-up walls are loaded in the laboratory to a presumed wind-load condition. On other buildings the calculation of strength could be described as more or less casual. Furthermore, there often are large differences between what is shown on the drawings and what is actually installed.

Owners generally buy curtain walls on

the basis of a performance specification along with certain profile information prepared by the architect. The specification probably says very little about "hardware," i.e. anchorages, etc., and sizes of supporting members. The fabricator then produces a technical design. He basically accepts the responsibility for the wall resisting the forces of nature. If something goes wrong and the manufacturer is a reputable one, presumably he will fix the deficiency.

Shouldn't responsibility for structural integrity be given more careful thought?

But if there were, say, a large number of failures during a catastrophic hurricane, what might the courts find? Perhaps they might find that because of so many failures, a norm had been established. On the other hand, how can non-professional organizations establish norms and standards? The norm is what the norm is, and maybe it was not good enough. Who in the end has to accept the financial responsibility?

Analysis of the basic structure of many types of curtain walls is simple applied mechanics.

Structural design of many types of curtain walls (stick systems, for example) is straightforward, easy to understand.

But very substantial safety factors should be used in the design of connections to allow for fatigue problems, corrosion, etc. With custom curtain walls, however, it is possible to overlook design problems by not clearly thinking through how they really work (particularly when there are conditions such as stone, glass, metal intersections; huge metal panels, etc.). These are areas where the structural engineer could get more deeply involved. Structural engineers with experience in tall buildings ought to be able to review the structural strengths of curtain wall components. The trouble, of course, is fees; current architectural fees do want to bear this cost because now this cost is borne outside. Further, engineers would have to take on responsibility in terms of costs, contingent liabilities, etc. The courts feel that when architects or engineers "dabble" in design, they must take the responsibility for it.

How wise is it to continue to leave the responsibility for technical design and performance with the manufacturer? First of all, who else is there to do it? But is a better discipline needed within the industry? The industry is tremendously large, and there are many firms in it. What can be done to help ensure that all firms act responsibly? Trouble is it is easy for a firm to go into the business because not much capital is required, at least for the common types of curtain walls. There tends to be a big turnover of companies; and there are those who do not have a good overall knowledge of the field. Further, even the better companies have difficulty in finding competent technical personnel today.

There are more problems today with curtain walls than there ought to be. Rain gets through, occasionally glass is broken, and, more rarely, curtain wall panels are torn off by wind.

Because the modern curtain wall has existed for 20 years or more, one might presume that all the problems have been solved. Not so! Granted that much knowledge has been acquired, and that new materials have proliferated. But cost pressures have forced manufacturers to fabricate products that are closer and closer to minimum safety factors, with little margin for contingencies — such as if service conditions turn out to be more severe than those stipulated in the criteria.

The answer lies in architects being able to pin down performance requirements more precisely and more thoroughly. And, they must have available to them the technical expertise for evaluating manufacturers' designs, proposals and costs. Because of this need, independent curtain wall consultants have begun to emerge. Some architects who do a lot of custom curtain wall work may find it advisable to develop in-house expertise in some areas of curtain wall design and technical evaluation.

What the architect should recognize is that owners are becoming more and more aware of curtain wall problems, and they will find means to prevent them, if no one else does. It will be better for everyone if the architect understands why curtain wall problems exist and takes steps to prevent them through carefully prepared specifications, competent evaluation of proposals, and knowledgeable inspection of work in the field.

Curtain wall specifications often are poorly written today. One of the reasons for this is that many architects derive much of their specification content from industry standards and manufacturers' information without understanding as much as they should about the basis for this material and its limits. This becomes even more important as performance specifications are used more frequently.

In using performance specifications, the architect needs to be very specific about performance criteria in both qualitative and quantitative terms. It is no substitute to rely, instead, heavily on manufacturers' guarantees—for example, including in the general conditions section a broad statement such as, "This building shall remain watertight for five years, and the manufacturer shall make all repairs that are necessary." While such a statement may seem to provide protection by fixing responsibility, all is for nought if the building leaks—the owner is unhappy, the architect is in trouble, the manufacturer is in trouble, and the occupant is in trouble. A guarantee doesn't help if the architect has not tied down performance criteria carefully, and the manufacturer does not understand fully the environmental conditions to which the wall will be subjected. And if performance requirements are not pinned down, what one manufacturer feels is acceptable may not be the same as another manufacturer's concept. Obviously, responsible manufacturers want to avoid a malfunctioning system because repair costs can be tremendous—at times almost prohibitive.

Once a tight set of performance criteria has been developed, every effort should be bent toward defining the system in mechanical terms, with a system that meets those criteria being described in as complete and clear detail as possible. For example, in a good performance specification, allowable wall erection tolerance, expansion tolerances, and deflections will be pinned down. Deflection will not be given merely as, say, 1/175 of the span, but as the maximum allowable in inches; the maximum operating temperature range will be given, etc. In other words, the spec-

ification relates a specific curtain wall to a specific structure. Further, erection procedures need to be spelled out. A properly written performance specification provides an equitable basis for bidding for manufacturers of similar quality levels. In the past some specifications have restricted bidding by being too proprietary. If, for example, the joinery is defined too specifically, this could favor one manufacturer to the exclusion of others, even though it might not matter whether a window is screwed together, welded, or mortised and tenoned, if it performs structurally and weatherwise, and meets appearance requirements.

Quality varies depending upon the type of client and the architect's approach

Obviously, the building owner has the responsibility in establishing the level of quality he wants in a building—speculative building vs. owner-built building. Some owners, particularly developers of speculative buildings, may want to accept a certain amount of maintenance on a curtain wall rather than paying more money for a better one. It is possible that the owner might want the flexibility of having alternate glazing systems for bidding. If this be the case, the architect should represent the entire range from top to bottom that is acceptable, and these alternates should be developed by the architect, not the manufacturer. The architect should define minimum level of performance in mechanical terms. Then the situation wouldn't arise in which the architect designs a "Cadillac" and the owner goes out and buys a "Ford." The owner thought he was buying a "Cadillac," because all the systems looked the same.

With prestigious buildings, an architect may prefer to fully detail the custom curtain wall and glazing systems, provided that he has had the experience and has knowledgeable personnel available to him to carry through. He needs to be certain of his performance criteria and needs to be sure how they can be answered. While this approach limits the options available to the supplier, it means that most likely the architect should have no "surprises" with respect to performance.

The functional integrity of a curtain wall is as important as its architectural expression

The first step toward getting a curtain wall that works is the preparation of a set of highly developed performance criteria. Then the system needs to be described in mechanical terms (i.e., type of anchorages, weep system, thickness of glass, etc.) in as complete and clear detail as is possible.

The architect's in-house costs are high the first time he uses a new approach—butted glass for example. It may not always involve new technology, but development of criteria can take time.

Prequalification of bidders makes it more likely that proposals are comparable

There are advantages to all parties in prequalifying manufacturers who have equivalent capabilities for a certain type of building in a certain location. These manufacturers might be asked to submit proposal drawings along with detailed information and calculations. The architect, then, will know not only the price, but what the manufacturer plans to produce. The advantage to manufacturers is they are competing with their peers. Obviously prequalification will only work if all the manufacturers really do have equivalent competence and capability. If this is not adhered to and other companies are let in, brand "X" may fall far below others; then manufacturers "A," "B," and "C" may put in only token bids because they know they cannot meet brand "X's" price. The architect should keep in mind that some manufacturers are not able to provide the same quality in different locations of the country, but, say one quality in New York, another in Chicago, and still another on the West Coast because of different manufacturing facilities, different staffs, etc.

Standards are not a bench-mark of quality because they are based on minimum levels

Because a great many of the standards in the curtain-wall field are developed by manufacturers' trade organizations, they are, perforce, minimum standards. While they say that most products should try to achieve higher levels, cost pressures force maximum quality down to minimum standards. Example: manufacturer "A" has a window that falls within a given classification of a standard, and is at the top end of the spectrum. Manufacturer "B's" window has lesser capabilities, but still falls within the same classification; obviously manufacturer "A" is not competitive.

Some standards are deficient because the tests that are used are geared to laboratory application, rather than being equated to field use, and correlation is not made between the two.

Architects should realize also that some standards cover test methods only and do not indicate quality levels. For example, if performance levels are alluded to in an ASTM specification, these are given to indicate application of the standard and are not performance parameters; the user must specify whatever performance level he feels is necessary for the building he is designing.

Architects and engineers need to have standards clarified so that they understand their basis and intent of use. That such clarification is needed is obvious in that often specifications are found to be comprised largely of excerpts pulled out from various standards; they may even have been paraphrased and interchanged in such a manner that they make no sense at all. They are used, despite lack of understanding, undoubtedly because the person who prepares the specification feels this offers a certain degree of protection.

Further, some standards are used in curtain wall specifications that were never intended to be applied to large, high-rise buildings that experience the more severe weather conditions. Independent consultants such as L. J. Heitmann of St. Louis state that, in general, all standards need to be upgraded. It is entirely possible today for, say, half a dozen manufacturers to comply with a given test, but the performance levels of their products may be totally different, while in theory they are all equal. Heitmann says the architect should realize that for many of his designs, he cannot accept the minimum levels called for today. Undoubtedly, too, manufacturers would like to see better standards, particularly if they helped everybody to compete on the same basis.

Some existing standards, on the other hand, serve their purpose satisfactorily; standards on finishes are an example. But in this category there is not the chance for ambiguity that there is with techniques of joining, fabrication and assembly—all of which affect performance levels as well as costs.

The technical expertise for design and costing exists; question is how to get it

When an architectural firm is large enough, and they do enough of the same kinds of buildings, they can develop in-house expertise, but they have to be able to move their expert from job to job in order to afford him. A specialist can get involved in the preliminaries—setting standards, the pace of the job, etc. Doubtless there is very little that the office of Emery Roth & Sons doesn't know about making a curtain wall effective. Irving Gershon of that office starts out assuming that the curtain wall may leak someplace, and that means are necessary for trapping water and redirecting it to the outside: gutters, weep holes, baffles to keep wind from blowing in.

Smaller offices, obviously have to depend more upon outside sources for technical expertise.

The 25-man office of Bower & Fradley, architects in Philadelphia, has found it advantageous to bring in an outside cur-

The level of performance that the curtain wall should achieve must be established by the architect

Obviously, there will be a range of quality levels for curtain walls in a variety of buildings. The desired level must be decided between owner and architect. In control of quality via the specification, the architect should understand the intent, implications and applicability of standards.

tain wall consultant. First of all, their experience is that in the last five years or so, manufacturers have not been able to spend as much time as formerly in working out curtain wall problems. Further, they find that an outside consultant can save in-office time and help make sure the specification is more precise. For example, architects find it difficult to keep up with sealant technology; specifying color range has to be precise to get the results the architect and his client want.

What kinds of services can a curtain wall consultant provide? L. Russell Buczkowski of Peter Corsell Associates, Inc. of New York reports that their involvement with the architect often begins with design conception, and is followed by development of performance critieria; definition of the mechanical systems involved (anchorage, glazing system, etc.); developing methods of analyzing and testing wall systems; reviewing proposed systems and advising on the acceptability and cost value of the proposed system. Once the contract is awarded and a system is defined, the firm reviews it with regard to structural and mechanical aspects and water-leakage control. Periodically they inspect fabrication at the manufacturer's plant, spot-checking for color control, fabrication tolerances, shop fabricating techniques such as welding and sealing. One of the functions of the consultant is to protect the owner on costs—to see that he gets what he pays for and within the scope of what the architect has defined.

The way curtain wall contracts are negotiated these days, Buczkowksi says, it is critical that those doing the negotiating for the owner and evaluating proposals by suppliers be completely aware of the technical aspects of the systems so that lines can be drawn beyond which no com-

promises will be made, so as to ensure the proper level of quality. Further, some means of evaluating pricing should be available to the owner so that he gets an equitable price. An example might be when a supplier wants to, for example, substitute lighter extrusions for the wall, but provide additional anchorages—obviously such change needs to be evaluated both tecnically and cost-wise.

Another curtain-wall consultant L. Jack Heitmann Jr. of the St. Louis consulting engineering firm of L. H. Antoine & Associates offers many years of experience as head of technical services for a major curtain wall manufacturer. His firm's services include: 1) selection of suppliers; 2) preparation of specifications and general scope drawings (asking for proposals drawings with bids that show evidence of meeting specifications); 3) critiquing bids and awarding contracts; 4) supervision of mock-up testing, 5) field inspection and testing (e.g., testing for leakage with a hose).

Testing for the structural integrity of glass and curtain wall assemblies is one of the functions provided by another consulting engineering firm—Wiss, Janney & Elstner of Chicago (North Plains, Illinois). They have, for example, tested large, reflective double-glazed units for solar load followed by sudden chilling.

Building Materials Research Institute of New York gained a lot of early experience in sealants with curtain wall and glazing applications. Early on, much of their work dealt with investigating failures, but now more is new work involving, in part, field quality control aspects.

Full-scale mock-up tests, including the simulation of wind-driven rain, are performed by Construction Research Laboratory in Miami, headed by A. A. Sakhnovsky, but these have limitations.

Mock-up testing has its place, but the similitude to reality must be considered

How well does the mock-up test relate to actual conditions? That is the big question. Are you testing what you are going to see erected in the field; and are you testing in a manner indicative of the exposure you are going to have? In many cases the tests are limited in terms of the size of the mock-up and the exposure criteria that determine the tests. For example, consultants say, differential wind load tests about the center line of the spandrel are very seldom run to determine whether there is any rotation about the anchors or undue deflection of members caused by unsymmetrical loading. Further, there are high negative loadings on some areas of buildings—as a result, some spandrel panels and column covers have been lost.

Further, testing may be curtailed on a mock-up if, for example, a light of glass breaks due to damage in installation, and only the positive wind loading has been completed, but not the negative. In such a case, the anchorages have not been tested for negative loading.

Not too much emphasis can be put on the point that what is shown in shop drawing and what is erected in the building may or may not be the same. A fabricator may change an extrusion or an anchorage—not grossly, but perhaps in some important details. Granted that the manufacturer accepts the responsibility for the structural integrity of the curtain wall if he is guaranteeing it according to performance specifications, but the architect is not free of difficulties, particularly if there is a failure.

So what needs to be done to upgrade the end product—buildings?

First of all there needs to be more comprehensive and careful definition of the technical areas involved in the design and fabrication of curtain walls—by owner, architect, manufacturer. The field needs to be more clearly understood in an over-all sense by the people who buy the product. The true basis for negotiating a curtain wall contract needs to be understood from a technical aspect. And finally, the architect needs to have a thorough enough acquaintance with the technical aspects of curtain wall design and construction, and to have the right kind of technical support, so that a properly working curtain wall system can be designed and constructed that is within the owner's budget.

Procedure that a large architectural firm uses to control strength of glass

Fazlur R. Kahn, partner and chief structural engineer of Skidmore, Owings & Merrill, Chicago lists three steps the firm takes in designing and checking the glass installation:

Step I:

1. Check the local code. Is it realistic in terms of statistical analysis of winds according to weather records (50-100 year recurrence velocity; profile up to 1000 ft)?

2. If the building is an average, rectangular one, use judgment for assigning pressure coefficients for corner zones and the interior zones of building faces. Zone the building for every 100 ft of height.

3. Use a safety factor of 2 and 100-yr recurrence wind. Pressure equals velocity^2 $\times$ 0.00256 $\times$ shape factor $\times$ gust factor^2. (PPG literature says the minimum shape factor for a building is 1.25, but that in some cases, values as high as 5 may be appropriate for certain areas of a building.) If code values are higher, then they supersede.

4. If the building shape is unusual, or if over 50 stories, or if the site situation is unusual (e.g., tunnel effect), the engineers recommend that a wind tunnel test be employed. Pressures are checked every 5 degrees for all 360 degrees.

Step II:

Run a full-scale mock-up test of an assembly with mullions and glass simulating actual building details and glazing details. Glass is selected on the basis of a safety factor of 2. The assembly is said to pass if it withstands 1.5 times design load (obviously, the frame cannot be infinitely stiff). Gaskets, if used, are checked for possible roll-off: bite, neoprene hardness, width of gasket (are any of these insufficient?). How is the bite with metal stops? Stiffness of mullions is important. Deflection equal to 1/175, per se, is meaningless; amount permissible will be dependent upon size and shape of glass light, proportions and exact details of stops.

Step III:

Review shop drawings. Make field measurements and reports—tolerances, opening sizes, squareness of frames. Make visual observations of glass. (For example on the Sears building in Chicago, glass is to be checked as follows: 1st typical floor, 50 per cent; 3rd typical floor, 50 per cent; remaining typical floors, 5 per cent.)

The provision of quality-control measures—or the lack of them—can greatly affect performance of curtain-wall systems. Testing at an independent laboratory to the effectiveness of a curtain wall against wind-driven rain is shown below, left. When erection quality is not specified, or is not checked adequately in the field, conditions can result as shown below, right—an opening badly out of square.

Opitimizing the Structure of the Skyscraper: Examples from SOM in Chicago show a clear, logical progression in structure and its expression, as skyscrapers go up and up

The Chicago office of Skidmore, Owings & Merrill, located in the city where the skyscraper originated, is taking this architectural form to new-found heights, and in the process is producing architectural forms that express the rationality of the structural systems, and that exploit their planning potentialities.

Early skeleton frames still carried heavy loads of masonry, though the exterior walls merely supported their own weight. Wind load was not much of a problem then, but it became one when buildings shed their heavy masonry skins, and the structures had to do all the work.

When buildings are not very high, rigidly connected beams and columns can carry the wind. But the post-and-beam approach becomes inefficient after about 20 stories. Other systems that supplant post-and-beam also reach limits in efficiency as they reach greater heights.

The result is that as structures have thrust higher—20, 40, 60, 100, 110 stories—

new families of structural systems have evolved, each suitable for given ranges of heights in steel, concrete, or their combination.

What these families of systems are can be seen most clearly in the work of the Chicago office of SOM over the past decade. Their achievements in the skyscraper genre stem from the unique combination of individuals, plus the emphasis put on very early collaboration between engineers and architects. And it can do so because of having both strong engineering and architecture inputs in-house. Discussions start when only the building program is more or less known —and nothing has even been sketched. Architecture and engineering are then discussed together to try to synthesize them into a coherent building form.

The buildings and structures that then emerge from the SOM office are a result not only of this philosophy, but also of the types of people involved: the structural engineer has to be somewhat of an architect, and the

architect somewhat of an engineer. A very close interaction between their thoughts must occur.

A case in point is Sears Tower. The bundled tube structural concept Fazlur Khan developed meshed with design partner Bruce Graham's search for a shape that could gradually drop off floor areas as the building rose higher, to give the different sizes of floors the client wanted.

Khan feels that teaching is a very important part of his professional life—the work with students helping to stimulate new ideas and concepts, as well as to think them through. He proudly points to the high competence-level of engineers in his department—attributing a high efficiency of output, in conceptual and technical terms, to this fact. He believes the engineer's role, as the architect's, is to make solutions as simple and as direct as possible. He has proved that out of simple logic and simple structural solutions, good and great, architectural forms can develop

The architect seeks a flexible, uncluttered plan, and an economic height; the engineer seeks the simplest way to bring loads down to the ground

When the skyscrapers really began to go "up" in numbers and height in Chicago about 10 years ago, significant changes in structural design approaches began to emerge from the office of Skidmore, Owings & Merrill, there. Even before that in 1958, the firm produced a bold, husky expression for Inland Steel's 60-ft-clear-span rigid frame of 19 stories. Three years later saw the 20-story Hartford Building which gave a clear, strong expression of a concrete flat plate design in 22-ft-square bays. Then in 1964, SOM stretched the bay sizes to 36 ft in the 19-story BMA building in Kansas City. The rigid-frame steel structure is welded, and high-strength steel was used in the 36-ft-long girders. Projecting in front of the glass, the structure is one of the clearest expressions of a steel rigid frame.

In a frame structure, the total lateral drift caused by wind is due to two primary factors: 1) bending moments in the girders (65 per cent of the total), and bending moments in the columns (15 per cent); and 2) axial stresses due to the overturning moment, resulting in column shortening and lengthening (20 per cent). Obviously drift has to be controlled to prevent undue wracking of partitions and windows, and to avoid building movement being unpleasantly perceptible to the occupants.

Fazlur Khan, partner and chief structural engineer of SOM, Chicago, has demonstrated in a number of technical papers that the structural performance of a rigid frame can be improved when a vertical shear truss or shear wall is combined with it. The drawings below show that the frame tends to pull back the shear truss or wall in the upper portion of the building, and push it forward in the lower portion. As a result, the frame is more effective in the upper portion where the wind shears are less (they go from zero at the top and build up to maximum at the base), and the shear wall or truss carries most of the shear in the lower portion of the building, where the frame cannot afford to carry high lateral load. This construction in which the shear truss interacts with the frame has been used in a number of buildings in the 40-story range.

For example in the Chicago Civic Center (C. F. Murphy and SOM, associated architects), the upper half of the building is a pure rigid frame construction, while the lower half is a shear truss-interaction structure. When a rigid frame is combined with a shear truss, the lateral sway is frequently reduced to 50 per cent of that if the truss had been used alone, and, further, the distortion of the floors is less.

This same approach works in concrete, too, with the "shear truss" being replaced by a "shear wall." SOM's example here is the 38-story Brunswick building in downtown Chicago. Finished in 1962, it was one of the first major-size buildings in Chicago

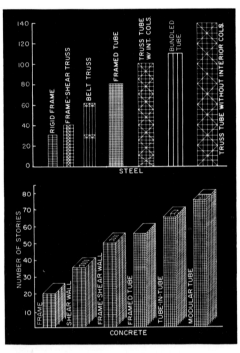

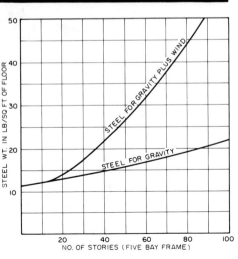

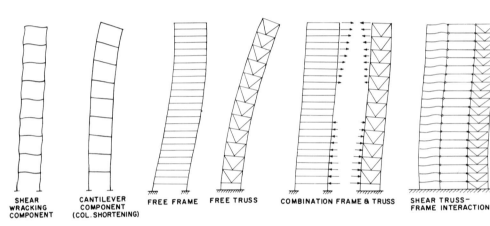

SHEAR WRACKING COMPONENT — CANTILEVER COMPONENT (COL. SHORTENING) — FREE FRAME — FREE TRUSS — COMBINATION FRAME & TRUSS — SHEAR TRUSS-FRAME INTERACTION

The taller buildings become, the stiffer they need to be to resist wind economically. The evolution of structures, including new concepts, to do this is shown, left. Low buildings up to 20 stories use rigid frames to limit sway, with wracking accounting for about 90 per cent of it. The 19-story BMA building (below) is a classic expression of a steel rigid frame. Because rigid frames are limber to some extent, they are inefficient for taller buildings. A first step to improve them is to add a shear truss (see above) which increases stiffness of the frame.

Ezra Stoller © ESTO

to be built after the Prudential building. The program called for deeper space than usual—a 38-ft span from perimeter to core. In plan there is a 38-ft free span, a 38-ft corridor, and then another 38-ft free span.

At first SOM's engineers thought that the structure would be designed so that the core's shear walls would carry all the wind load, while the columns would carry only gravity load. But because of the long clear spans, columns had to be closer together than ordinarily—in this case 9 ft 4 in. apart, which was double the building module, and equal to the size of a "minimum" office. Obviously the columns of the exterior wall would not just "sit there." Because the frame was concrete, the columns and beams had a natural continuity. In essence, then, the building had shear wall-frame interaction. As a matter of fact, the engineers determined that with the building designed, the shear walls alone would allow the building to drift 13 inches with the strongest wind. But combining the shear walls with rigid frame action, the drift would be reduced to only 3 inches.

Concrete was chosen because at that time it was on the order of $1 per square foot cheaper than steel. Further, the closely spaced columns and the spandrel beams provided a natural frame for the windows.

In order to create adequate spaces for entry to the building, the individual loads of the closely-spaced columns had to be picked up by a huge transfer girder, 24-ft high and 8-ft deep, supported by 7- by 7-ft columns spaced 56 ft apart. Though the girder was huge, it served well the problem of caisson-to-rock foundations, and the space behind it was used for location of the boiler and mechanical equipment.

A one-way joist type of slab was used between the exterior columns and the core, and this led naturally to a two-way waffle system at the corners. Because columns at the edge of the waffle are loaded more than the others, the columns were made deeper. Water riser details were manipu-

lated at the other columns to match the two deeper ones near the corners. In later SOM buildings, the columns have been allowed to project on the outside, forming part of the visual expression.

For steel buildings in the 50-story range, the efficiency of the structure has been increased by tying the exterior columns to the core with belt trusses

It was pointed out earlier that the rigid frame structure, with bays of fair size, is inefficient because of the bending in the columns and beams. This can be improved upon, however, by connecting all exterior columns to the interior shear truss by means of belt trusses, which can increase the stiffness of the structure by about 30 per cent. When the core tries to bend under wind load, the belt truss, acting like a lever arm, throws direct axial stresses into the columns—compression on one side, and tension on the other. (An outrigger truss of this type was used in the U.S. Steel

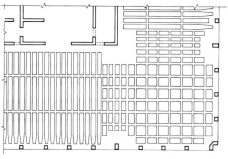

The shear truss is more effective at lower floors, where the loading effect of the wind is largest, because effect of cantilever bending there is least (see diagrams across page). In Chicago's Civic Center, above, wind is resisted by a shear truss, rigid-frame combination in the lower floors, and by the rigid frame, alone, in upper floors. A similar kind of structural behavior is obtained in concrete by using an exterior rigid frame working together with concrete shear walls in the core. This approach was used in 1962 in the Brunswick building in Chicago by SOM. The floor framing is a one-way joist system, except for the corners which are two-way waffle slabs. Columns at the transition between the one-way system and the waffle slab are larger because of carrying more waffle weight.

building and interior lateral trusses are being used in the I.D.S. building in Minneapolis—designed by other engineers).

Fazlur Khan first proposed belt trusses for the BHP Headquarters building in Melbourne, designing the structure for it. Comparative deflection curves for that building, with and without the belt truss system, are shown below. Obviously, the steel belt truss system at mid-height of the building contributes substantially to the stiffness of the building, as does the one at the top.

A similar system has been employed in the 42-story First Wisconsin Center in Milwaukee by SOM. Here, not only are belt trusses used at mid-height and at the top, but a truss at the bottom is used as a transition member to collect column loads.

Shear wall design long has been a means for stiffening apartment buildings up to 30 stories and office buildings up to 20 stroies or so. Studies for SOM projects have shown that over 30 stories, lateral sway as well as wind stresses begin to control the design, and structural elements designed only for gravity loads need to be made larger for stiffness and strength.

All approaches for optimizing tall skyscrapers have one thing in common: increasing the rigidity of the structure so it performs as a cantilevered tube

The floor plan of an apartment building wants to be more flexible than that of an office building; further the core is smaller, so it is better from these standpoints if the exterior walls alone could do the work in resisting wind, and that the shear walls be omitted. Maximum efficiency for lateral strength and stiffness, using the exterior wall alone as the wind-resisting element, can be achieved by making all column elements connected to each other in such a way that the entire building acts as a hollow tube cantilevering out of the ground.

Such a scheme was conceived in 1961 for the 43-story DeWitt Chestnut apartment building on Chicago's north side. The structure was thought of as a cantilevered tube with holes punched in it for windows, with smaller holes in the lower part and larger holes at the top because forces are less in the upper part. This tube was achieved in practice by having closely spaced columns (5 ft 6 in. centers) acting together with the spandrel beams, and this system is called the "framed tube."

The framed tube has limitations when used in buildings over 400 ft high because although the system looks like a tube, the two faces parallel to the wind act like a multi-bay rigid frame. As a result, the bending moments in the columns and edge beams become the controlling factor in unusually tall buidings. Further, of the total lateral sway, only about 25 per cent is due to column shortening caused by the cantilever action of the framed tube; 75 per cent is caused by frame wracking. The phenomenon is known as shear lag, and is shown at the bottom of page 183. Ideally the shear transfers should be a linear rela-

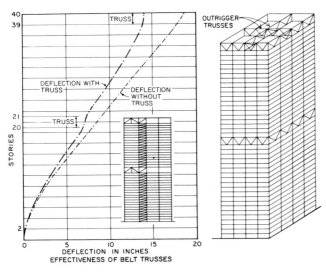

Above 40 stories the shear-truss, rigid-frame combination requires more and more steel for wind load. The effectiveness can be increased, however, by tying the shear truss to the exterior columns with belt trusses. The belt trusses, working as lever arms, throw direct axial stresses into the exterior columns. When the shear truss tries to bend, the exterior rows of columns act as struts to resist this movement. These belt trusses can be used not only at the top of the building, but midsection as well, increasing the stiffness of the building by 30 per cent. This approach has been used by SOM for the 42-story First Wisconsin Center in Milwaukee shown in the model photo below.

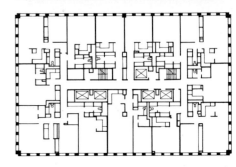

Rigid frames in concrete can be made more effective if the columns are spaced closely enough together so that the exterior structure works like a cantilevered tube when wind-loaded. The approach is especially favorable for apartment buildings, such as SOM's DeWitt Chestnut, in which core areas are small and planning flexibility is very desirable.

tionship; i.e., stresses in the building faces parallel to the wind should be direct tensions and compressions. But because of wracking of the frame, bending occurs, and columns at the corners of the building have to take more than their share of the load, while columns in between do less work than they ought to—so efficiency is reduced to the extent that beams and columns are limber, and consequently to the extent the frame wracks.

Framed tubes suffer from a problem called shear lag because the columns and beams bend when the wind blows. One remedy: stiffen the wall with diagonals

Exterior wall frames can be made stiffer and more rigid to mitigate wracking, however (and thus so-called shear lag). One method is to use diagonals in the wall, and, of course, the most striking example of this approach is the 100-story John Hancock building. The system used is the optimized column-diagonal truss tube. Ob-

viously the most effective tube action would be obtained by eliminating vertical columns and replacing them with closely spaced diagonals in both directions. But this not only presents problems in terms of window details and the large number of joints between diagonals, but the diagonals are less efficient than vertical columns in bringing gravity loads down to the ground. The column-diagonal tube, therefore, is an efficient compromise. The exterior columns have normal spacing, but are made to act together as a tube by the widely spaced diagonals. Except at levels where diagonals meet at corners of the building, the spandrels will resist the internal forces between columns and diagonals, but at these points it is necessary to provide a large tie spandrel to limit the horizontal stretching of the floors, and to make the diagonals function more efficiently as inclined columns, and as primary load-distribution members.

A similar approach can be worked out in concrete, as well. With the rigid tube

type of design it should be possible for concrete buildings to go 70, 80, even 100 stories. In contrast, with conventional beam and column framing, the practical height limit is on the order of 20 stories.

One way the rigidity can be achieved is with the column-diagonal approach. The diagonals can be created by filling in what normally would be windows in a diagonal pattern. With a rectangular building the diagonals will not cross on the wider faces, but they need to on the narrower faces for efficient transfer of wind load. Symmetry occurs about the corners, but not the faces of the building.

Still another approach in concrete that produces nearly 100 per cent rigidity is the interior bracing of the tube. A wall grid of closely-spaced columns is in effect "glued" to cross shear walls, so that the wall grid acts like the "flange" of a huge "beam," and shear walls act like "webs." Shear lag would be minimized, and stresses in the walls would be primarily axial.

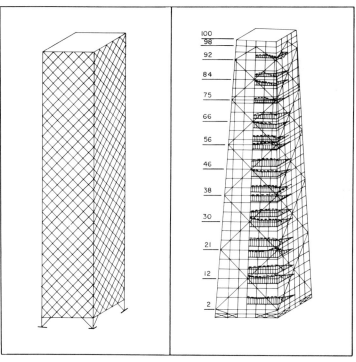

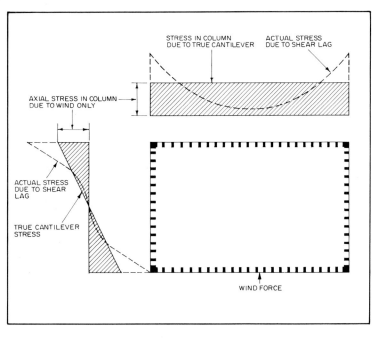

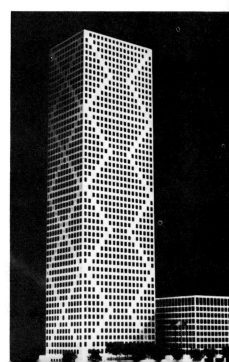

"Framed tube" is the designation given to structures that use closely-spaced columns in the exterior wall for wind load. But efficiency of framed tubes drops off in taller buildings (about 50 stories in concrete, 80 stories in steel). Ideally, columns and beams of a rigid frame would be infinitely stiff. But because these elements bend, a phenomenon occurs called, "shear lag," illustrated at left. Columns near corners do more work than they should; the others less. Shear lag can be greatly reduced by stiffening up the exterior; the stiffest means would be to replace vertical columns with diagonals. A more optimum approach from standpoints of overall efficiency and practicalness is to combine columns and diagonals as in the 100-story John Hancock building.

Efficiency of the framed tube can be improved if the interior core is also a tube, or if the exterior walls are braced by cross stiffeners

This scheme was used in a hypothetical 92-story apartment building by one of Fazlur Khan's students at Illinois Institute of Technology. For the system to work the shear walls have to be relatively continuous. With apartments having only an 8 ft 8 in. floor to floor height, openings in the shear wall for corridors could not be all in a vertical line because the shear wall "web" would be too weak. The problem is solved by using two different floor plans for alternate floors so that corridors, and thus openings, are staggered floor-to-floor.

A model was built in plastic, load tested, and found to be amazingly efficient. The system appears so simple and efficient that its actual application in an ultra-high rise building seems inevitable one of these days.

It has been shown that a concrete rigid frame and shear walls could interact to improve the performance of both, as in the Brunswick building. Going a step further, if the exterior wall is comprised of closely spaced columns so that it performs as a tube, and shear walls at the core also work as a perforated tube, then the structure becomes a "tube within a tube." The framed tube and shear wall-frame interaction concepts have been combined, and Fazlur Khan used this approach with the 52-story One Shell Plaza building in Houston. The building, at 715 ft, is the world's tallest reinforced concrete building, and the tube-in-tube concept made it possible at the unit price of a 35-story shear wall structure. The entire system is so efficient that all columns, shear walls and floors need be sized only for gravity loads. As with Brunswick, one-way joist system was used, in this case spanning 40 ft from exterior to core; columns were spaced 6 ft apart. The corners are a two-way waffle slab, and again, as in Brunswick, exterior columns near the corners of the waffle are more heavily loaded by gravity than the other columns. But, in contrast to Brunswick, these columns get gradually deeper, the additional depth is allowed to project out from the face in the building, and this gravity-load-carrying picture is expressed "plastically" in the building's exterior. In further contrast to Brunswick, the base of the building is pierced by much smaller openings, and the bold, massive base itself gathers up the columnar loads.

Such a tall building would not have been possible in Houston—because of poor soil conditions—if the structural engineers had not searched out the possibilities of high-strength lightweight concrete in the range of 6,000 psi for the entire structure. With conventional stone concrete, 35 stories would have been about the limit.

Further, the plan shape was changed from an original 120 by 240 ft (a tremendous "sail" area for Houston's 40 lb per sq ft wind load) to 192 ft by 132 ft—a ratio of

Ezra Stoller © ESTO photos

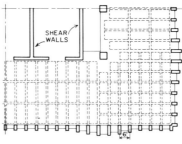

The concrete framed tube can be improved by making a structural tube out of the shear walls. The approach—called "tube-in-tube" was used for the 52-story One Shell Plaza. A picture of the increasing gravity loads in the columns next to the waffle slab can be seen in the undulated exterior. Increasing sophistication in collection of gravity loads of exterior columns is manifested in both One Shell Plaza, left and above, and in Rochester's Marine Midland bank, right. In the former, a massive base is pierced for access. In Marine Midland, the structure grows like a tree at the base.

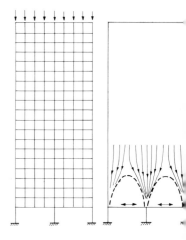

1:1.45 rather than 1:2. The foundation consists of a concrete mat sitting 60 ft below ground; it is over 8-ft deep and projects out 20 ft from the perimeter of the super-structure.

Funneling the gravity loads of closely spaced columns into wider-spaced columns at the base in the structural design also makes possible new visual expressions

Collecting the columnar gravity loads by means of a deep transfer girder is rather a brute-force approach, inasmuch as the girder has to work in inefficient post-and-beam fashion. So, more recently, SOM's architects and engineers have taken a closer look at the load flow in a rigid wall of closely-spaced columns, supported by widely-spaced columns at the base. The natural load flow is for columns to gradually shed their load toward the base columns. The wall, in effect, actually works as an arch. Recognizing this, SOM has done several buildings in which columns and spandrel beams grow larger as they approach the base columns. The most sophisticated of these buildings so far is the Marine Midland Bank building in Rochester in which each individual grid element up to the 6th floor is shaped so as to define and express the structural strength to take the flow of forces. The result is an expression akin to traditional bearing wall arches.

In steel buildings, the column-diagonal frame provides the most rigid tube, and this type of building acts most nearly like a cantilever sticking out of the ground as it is loaded by wind. But what if the owner doesn't want diagonals in the exterior wall? This was the problem that SOM faced when it was decided that the Sears headquarters would take the shape of a tower structure rather than a 42-story, but larger-plan building (130,000 sq ft per floor). After this, a two-building scheme was also considered—one 60 stories high, and the other 40 stories. In any event, Sears management wanted on the order of 50,000 sq ft per floor for their own use, but smaller floor areas were felt desirable for rental tenant spaces. The final choice—as is well known—was a building of nine bays, 75 by 75 ft, or a building 225 by 225 ft at ground level. Beyond the first 50 stories (which Sears is taking) the building peaks in sets of bays, with two bays rising the last 20 stories to the F.A.A. limit of 1,450 ft at 110 stories. Total gross area is 4.4 million sq ft.

Achieving efficient frames in ultra-high buildings without using stiffening diagonals has led to the bundled tube concept, with great planning flexibility

SOM's design partner for Sears, Bruce Graham wanted to create an open, pleasant space for the plaza level which implied a tall building rather than a squat one that would take the whole site. Engineer Fazlur Khan was sympathetic to the "environment" idea, but also wanted to achieve a tall building at lower-building costs. And

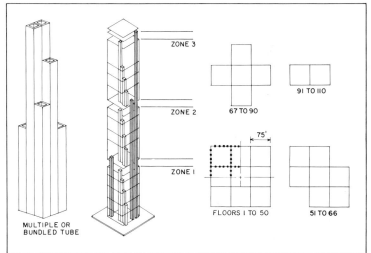

Perhaps the most intriguing concept to evolve in the ultra-high skyscraper — from both architectural and engineering aspects—is the one known as the "bundled-tube" approach, which was conceived for use in the 110-story Sears Tower. The building consists of a series of framed tubes, each of which has its own structural integrity, allowing the tubes to be dropped off as the building rises, yielding a variety of spaces for tenant floors which occur above the 50th floor. The tubes are 75-ft square, so the building is 225 by 225 ft at the base. Columns are optimally spaced 15 apart. At each corner of the tubes is a larger column that "terminates" the tube structurally with respect to wind shear transfer. Shear lag is greatly reduced, compared with an ordinary framed tube, as illustrated at right. The elevator system is divided into three zones, with two-story sky lobbies serving the double-deck elevators from the two lower zones. Sky lobbies also are served by express banks.

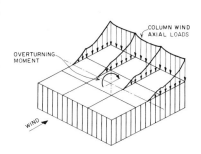

Robert E. Fischer

Graham was looking for a structural system that would let him drop off floor areas, so that part of the building would continue to rise in a prismatic way, but not the whole floor area.

With the shear-lag problem in mind, the idea occurred to Khan of putting two cross-stiffener frames (diaphragms) in each direction that would divide the building into nine cells. Then, as the building soared, cells could be dropped off, with others remaining independent. Cell size was one question. But a more important one, structurally, was that of column spacing. As the spacing gets very close (8-, 6-, 4-ft) the cost of steel and fabrications goes way up. But if columns are spaced more than 15 ft apart, the frame no longer works as a tube. So a spacing had to be found where the cost was least, but tube action would still exist. By many parametric studies (a number of simple equations and studies) it was found that 15-ft spacing worked well, while at the same time being in accord with the building module. Computer studies showed that shear lag was greatly reduced, and that there was very little premium in square-foot costs for height. Further, there was no need to use an extremely high-strength steel (50,000 psi was highest).

With the Sears type of structure, which has been called the "bundled-tube," shear lag occurs, but it takes place in segments, which has the effect of squashing the peaks of direct stresses in the columns. What happens is that, as far as shear lag is concerned, each of the tubes appears to act independently, and the shear lag diagram drapes (like a transmission line does) from the peak at the corners, to lesser and lesser heights to the center of the building.

Because the individual tubes are independently strong with respect to wind load, they can be bundled in any sort of configuration and dropped off at will, as the building rises higher. They could be bundled five in a row and still be efficient; or placed with four around a central tube (cruciform); or have two tubes by four tubes (an L-shape). With the tube concept there is a new vocabulary of architectural space possibilities.

SOM found that concrete tube-in-tube systems, while efficient in terms of materials, were diminished in a practical sense because of the time involved to produce poured-in-place construction.

They had to find a system that has the advantages of a concrete building, but not the disadvantages. One way to eliminate the disadvantage was to make the inside of the building steel, and only the outside (lateral-stability) portion a concrete grid. What has happened is that the framed tube concept has been combined with the traditional steel frame. So far the concrete exterior frames have been made using traditional formwork as well as with precast concrete forms that were left in place to form the finished exterior. Cost savings have been $1 to $1.50 per sq ft over all-concrete buildings.

The different types of floor plans that result from "dropping off" of bundled tubes are shown below. The upper plan of Zone 3 is the observation floor. In each of the zones, except for the top, are clear-span spaces, 75 by 75 ft. The curtain-wall system expresses the tubular nature, but not the framing of each of the tubes. While the tubes have been bundled in this particular configuration for Sears Tower, many others are possible, depending upon planning requirements. The ultimate structure, for structural efficiency, would appear to be a bundled tube with diagonals in the walls for increased stiffness.

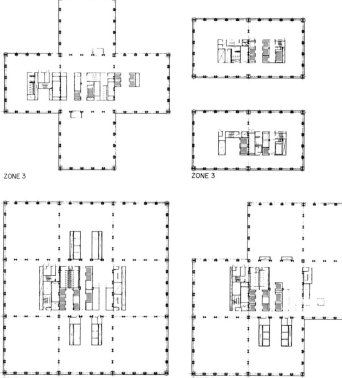

ZONE 3

ZONE 3

ZONE 1

ZONE 2

Research leads to a bolder expression of the steel frame

The strong, bold lines of the 54-story One Liberty Plaza in Manhattan's Lower West Side stand out in sharp contrast to its blander neighbors. First of all, the building is a design statement; but more than that, it is an experiment in the use of steel—all within the constraints of speculative building costs. The building is a design statement because its initiator and part-owner United States Steel wanted one. But also they wanted costs kept down because it is an investment building for them as well as for the major tenant, Merrill Lynch Pierce Fenner & Smith, and the developer, Galbreath-Ruffin.

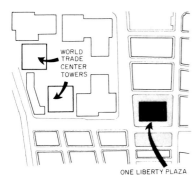

Seeking to stimulate innovation and progressive design in buildings made of steel—and in this one in particular—U. S. Steel commissioned the New York office of Skidmore, Owings & Merrill and their consultants, in a separately-financed study from the building design, itself, to, "investigate the design and use of materials in all phases of high-rise office building construction." Weidlinger Associates and Weiskopf & Pickworth were joint venture structural engineers; in the final design Weidlinger was responsible for the wind-bracing, while Weiskopf & Pickworth did the foundation design and the rest of the superstructure. Syska & Hennessy studied a wide variety of air-conditioning systems, lighting systems, and elevatoring. Galbreath-Ruffin Corporation reviewed design studies relating to rental efficiency, maintenance and operating costs. Turner Construction Company delved into erection systems and costs.

The time was propitious for investigation into structural possibilities because structural design of high-rise office buildings had begun to take some new directions—in wind-bracing, exterior bearing walls, and weight reduction. Further, research personnel at U. S. Steel's Applied Research Laboratory had produced studies that: 1) envisioned buildings with walls of plate steel that functioned efficiently as structure; and also that 2) suggested new approaches to the fire protection of the exterior steel framing

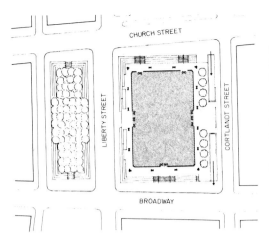

of high-rise buildings. Of nine prototype walls that were studied by SOM and their structural engineers, two involved steel-plate bearing walls, with each facade forming a "perforated monolithic steel plate devoid of columns or beams." Lack of fire testing of these schemes—which, obviously, would have had to be exceedingly exhaustive—plus uncertainties regarding costs, caused the elimination of these schemes.

On the other hand, theoretical fire studies by U. S. Steel's Applied Research Laboratory combined with actual fire tests led to the use of a new concept for protecting the spandrel plate girders which allowed a large portion of their exterior surface to be exposed to the weather. Flame canopies shield the outdoor side of spandrel girder flanges from excessive temperatures in the event of fire, and the outdoor side of the web has no fire protective material at all.

The building occupies a large percentage of its block-size site, allowed by the City Planning Commission because the owner was willing to develop an adjacent property as a small open-space park. Structurally, the building has

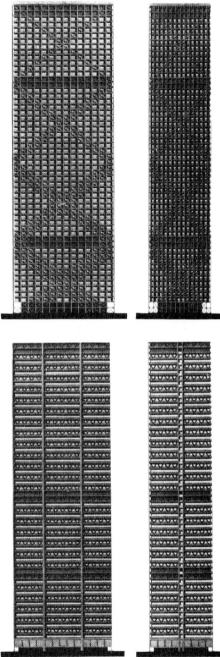

The three prototypes (out of nine) most favored for the frame, and hence for exterior expression are shown here. Fabrication costs were a negative factor for the Warren-truss prototype. This plus unresolved fire-protection problems of the exposed steel framing for both this scheme and the X-braced scheme led to the final selection of the rigid frame of husky columns and deep spandrels.

wide bays on the exterior and is clear span from exterior to core. The split-core plan— conceived to permit more efficient utilization of core-zone spaces—allowed wide, two-story-high trusses to be used in the core area for wind bracing in the narrow direction of the building. The rigid frame formed by deep plate-girder spandrels and heavy, built-up colums takes the wind load in the long direction, and part of it in the narrow direction.

While expressing the structural steel frame of a building is hardly new, the way it has been executed here definitely is new. Rather than being a cage-like expression, the spandrel girders are as high as the windows, and visually the flanges have been extended by the flame shields. This not only results in stronger accents in the facade, but functionally improves the sun-shading capability—just as deep reveals did in buildings of some years ago.

Of the nine structural framing schemes investigated, the three shown below in renderings were the most seriously considered. While the two that did not win out used less steel (particularly the X-braced scheme), higher fabrication and cladding costs of these schemes made the rigid-frame design selected more economical.

In one version, story-high Warren trusses, spanning 90 feet between columns, each supported two structural floors, one from the top chord and the other from the bottom. The diagonals of the trusses were connected by tension cables to give continuity for wind bracing.

In another version, small-bay X-bracing was oriented in a large X pattern, providing large-scale diagonal wind bracing to the exterior structural frame.

The X-braced prototype was found in the studies to have the least total cost for structure

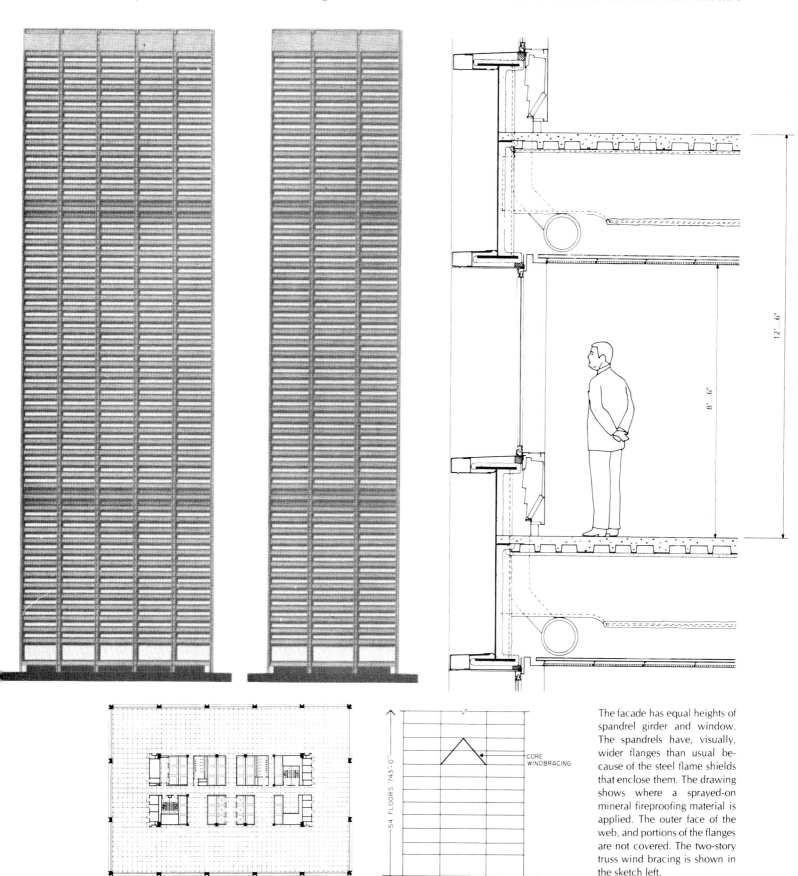

The facade has equal heights of spandrel girder and window. The spandrels have, visually, wider flanges than usual because of the steel flame shields that enclose them. The drawing shows where a sprayed-on mineral fireproofing material is applied. The outer face of the web, and portions of the flanges are not covered. The two-story truss wind bracing is shown in the sketch left.

because of dramatic savings in steel tonnage—about 50 per cent less than the structural system chosen, and over 40 per cent less than the Warren-truss system. But the architects' studies showed that savings in cladding costs for the scheme used more than offset the savings in the structural frame. Beyond this, there were unresolved problems with respect to fireprotecting the exterior frames of the two other prototypes.

Always looming in the picture, of course, are the hard realities (sometimes difficult for architects and engineers to swallow) of having to sacrifice theoretical efficiencies for heavier but lower-cost framing systems (and sometimes engineers would like to see more proof of this). In any event, for such buildings as this one, steel fabricators generally opt for larger and fewer pieces with fewer connections, in spite of the fact that tonnage is larger. This even applies to floor framing: at One Liberty Plaza, American Bridge preferred to cut a multiplicity of penetrations in the floor beams, rather than go to open-web trusses.

The exception, of course, appears to be the speculative skyscraper which does not call for a bold structural expression, and in which tenants are willing to put up with interior columns in rental space. Invariably these buildings tend to more closely spaced columns and thinner spandrels, using rolled, rather than built-up, sections.

Fire protection for the framing system selected for the building involved a combination of steel flame-impingement shields, size of windows and their location, and sprayed-on mineral-fiber fire-protective material. Spandrel girders have fireproofing on the interior side of the web and the outer faces of top and bottom flanges. Columns, on the other hand, are fully

The exposed steel webs, the flame shields over spandrel flanges and the steel column covers were all given a field coat of black paint on top of a zinc-paint primer. Joints are weather-protected by beads of sealant in a color that matches the paint.

The ground floor contains the lobby and various commercial spaces, while the second floor has a branch bank.

Flame shields are fastened to angles bolted to channels that are welded 4 ft 8 in. o.c. to the spandrel flanges. Column covers are bolted to the web of the spandrels. Sprayed-on mineral fireproofing covers all potentially vulnerable areas. Space between fireproofing and column cover has foamed-in-place urethane foam to minimize thermal movement of the columns.

coated with mineral fireproofing. The steel flame shields entirely cover the weather side of the spandrel flanges, and the columns are entirely encased with steel cladding. Column stiffeners are covered by the cladding, rather than being expressed, because of what this would have cost. And on the weather side, space between column fireproofing and the steel cladding is filled with foamed-in-place, urethane foam thermal insulation (it has a flame spread rating of less than 25). This insulation is necessary to limit thermal expansion and contraction of the exterior columns.

Additionally, the building department required firestopping at the spandrel girder-column connection.

The exterior—frame and cladding—were painted black in the field following prime coats of zinc paint, and black-pigmented sealant was applied to joints between the cladding and the exposed steel of the spandrel.

The horizontally pivoted windows—a U. S. Steel product—fill the vertical space between spandrels on all upper floors, and are attached to angles fastened to the flanges of the spandrel girders.

On the second floor, fixed sash is used because it is high-ceilinged and designed for commercial-space usage—Chase Manhattan Bank already occupies a large portion of the floor. This space was put on the second floor because the site drops rapidly in elevation from east to west. Originally the architects had conceived of the entire ground being open except for supporting columns and elevator shafts, but commercial considerations favored the total space being utilized.

The hvac system is more in a conventional, but nonetheless progressive, direction. Perime-

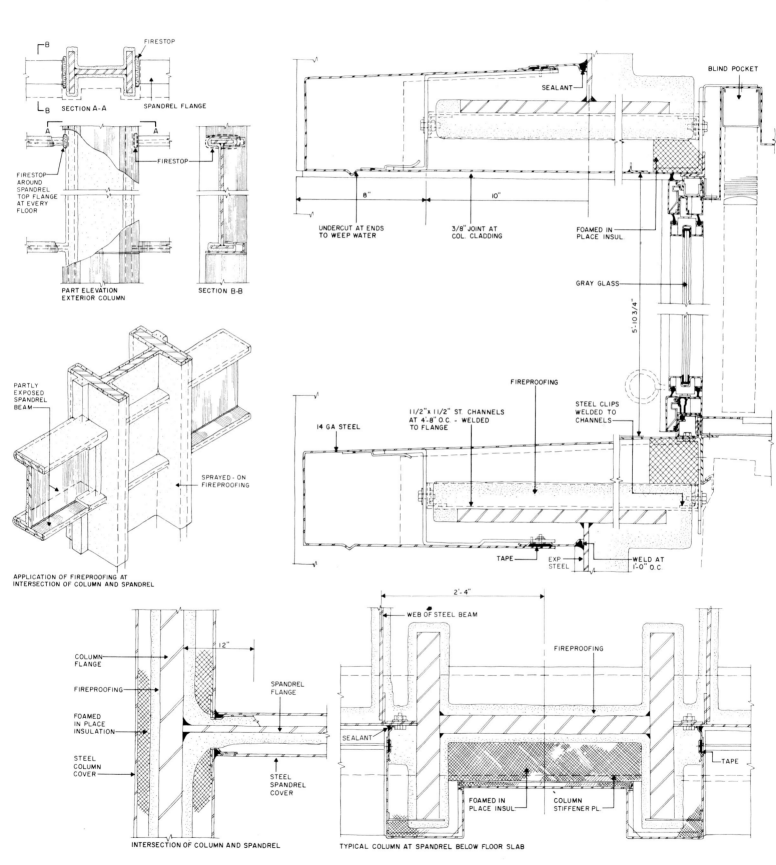

APPLICATION OF FIREPROOFING AT INTERSECTION OF COLUMN AND SPANDREL

INTERSECTION OF COLUMN AND SPANDREL

TYPICAL COLUMN AT SPANDREL BELOW FLOOR SLAB

ter areas are conditioned by an induction system, and interior zones by a variable-airvolume system. The building standard called for separate ceiling air diffusers for interior zones, but tenants, generally, are upgrading, visually, to air-supply-return type of lighting fixtures.

Because of the shallow space at columns, only water piping for the induction units is run there. Ductwork to serve them emanates from mechanical chases in the core and then turns laterally to feed induction units via penetrations through the floor. To provide enough room for the lateral ductwork, floor beams were notched in the bottom corner next to the spandrel.

Lighting is by 28- by 28-in., prismatic-lens luminaires with lampholders provided to take either two or three U-tube fluorescent lamps. Three-lamp units are put in a checkerboard. A number of pyramidal-coffer lighting systems using a variety of types of fluorescent and HID lamps were mocked up and costed, but the owners' economics favored the flat ceiling using perforated metal panels in the areas between luminaires. Prior to the commissioned research study, the engineers say, U-tube lamps had been used only for special sign lighting, and were produced only in Europe. But the engineers were able to induce manufacturers to bring them on the market here for interior building illumination.

ONE LIBERTY PLAZA, New York City, N.Y. Owner: Trinity Place Corporation. Architects: Skidmore, Owings & Merrill—partner-in-charge: Roy O. Allen; project manager: Walter A. Rutes; senior designer: Thomas G. Killian. Engineers: Weidlinger Associates and Weiskopf & Pickworth, joint venture (structural); Syska & Hennessy, Inc. (mechanical and electrical). General Contractor: Turner Construction Company. Developer: Galbreath-Ruffin Corporation.

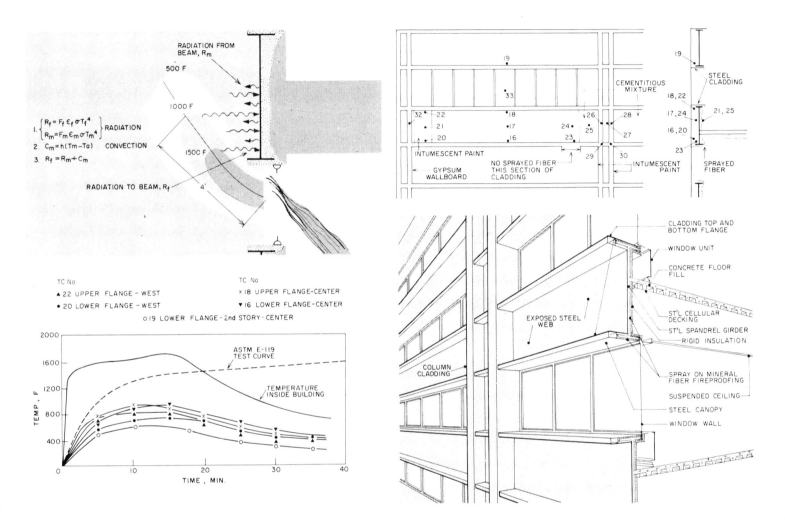

$$1. \begin{cases} R_f = F_f \, \epsilon_f \, \sigma \, T_f^4 \\ R_m = F_m \, \epsilon_m \, \sigma \, T_m^4 \end{cases} \text{RADIATION}$$

$$2. \quad C_m = h(T_m - T_\sigma) \quad \text{CONVECTION}$$

$$3. \quad R_f = R_m + C_m$$

The drawings on this page indicate the basis of the flame shield concept, and some results of fire tests on a one-bay mock-up. The idea of the shield on flanges is to deflect flame of a fire inside away from the spandrel.

The elevation shows location of thermocouples for measuring steel temperatures, and the graph indicates what some of these temperatures were. They all are below what is considered to be the safe limit for steel.

Columns always were intended to be protected by some fireproofing material, and to be covered with steel cladding.

SELECTED INTERIORS

The office interiors shown in this section represent a range of scales from the design of entire floors in modern office towers to the renovation of small nondescript spaces for the use of five or six persons.

The editorial offices of Doubleday and Company, Inc., in New York City occupy two entire floors of a typical Manhattan office high-rise, which were remodeled for their use within a stringent budget of approximately $10 per square foot between 1971-1972. To achieve their excellent results, the architects relied upon standard building materials and details, fabric prints and carefully selected colors.

The 20th and 21st floors of the Toronto-Dominion Centre (pages 107-116) are leased to the Aluminum Company of Canada, Ltd. In addition to using brilliant fabrics and colors in these headquarters, the architects have been highly inventive in their use of aluminum and aluminum products, combining this material with neon tubing and glass.

The design requirements of an architect's own office are similar to the requirements of most artists' and craftsmen's studios. Such spaces must be exceptionally well lit, have large amounts of storage space in which to order the inevitable clutter, and provide areas for design, drafting, model-making and business administration. Ideally, such spaces express order, neatness and efficiency, providing a serene ambience for creative and intellectual energies—as do the six architects' offices shown in this section.

DOUBLEDAY & COMPANY, INC.
EDITORIAL OFFICES, New York, New
York. Architect: *Jack Gordon*. Consultant: *Rosanne Gordon* (interiors).
Custom woodworking: *Unicraft Woodworking, Ltd.* Plantings: *Everett Conklin and Company Inc.* Contractor:
Edward Robbins, Inc.

Distinction need not hang on a
fortune, as proven here. When
Doubleday & Company moved its
offices to an existing midtown
Manhattan office tower, the company requested the architect, Jack
Gordon, to rehabilitate its two
floors within a stringent budget, in
this case approximately $10 per sq
ft. The two floors comprise 60,000
square feet. Eventually, five more
floors will be redesigned for a total
of 240,000 square feet.

Rather than use color as an
accent, the architect used it almost
structurally, to contain circulation
and work areas. The progression is
from neutral charcoal brown public and circulation areas, to white
work areas (right center).

To hold down costs, the architect chose to use building
standard materials and details. For
instance, the staircase at right (the
only structural change made),
connecting the two floors, features
stringer and treads of 2 by 10 in.
steel tube sections. Elsewhere, ordinary T-shaped ceiling spine is
used as a carpet stop and to create
reveals around door frames. The
result of such innovation is a custom-detailed job, at little cost.

To create different space experiences, the architect carpeted
the floors and walls of major circulation areas in charcoal brown.
The noise-absorbing quality of
carpet allowed the freedom to
eliminate ceiling-high walls and
substitute low partitioning. Since
the carpet also absorbs high light
levels where not needed, the work
areas seem brighter.

Because of cost factors again,
the concealed grid ceiling with 2
by 4 foot fluorescent fixtures had
to be retained. However, by rearranging the lights as the design required, the architect was able to
minimize an otherwise discordant
element. Existing metal and translucent glass partitions had to be
re-used for perimeter offices; but
thousands of feet of bank screen
were rejected in favor of the 5 foot
6 inch-high drywall partitions with
storage space in some (lower left
photo).

Bernard Askienazy photos

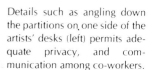

Details such as angling down the partitions on one side of the artists' desks (left) permits adequate privacy, and communication among co-workers.

A bright theme color was selected for each floor, first introduced on elevator doors, then carried into various departments. Fabric prints add inexpensive color to public areas. Orange is the code color for the 39th floor (plan shown) and yellow indicates the 38th floor.

Turning an economic necessity into a design asset, the architect used existing translucent glass partitions (above) in perimeter offices to let natural light into the personnel waiting area and secretary stations behind the bookcase partitions.

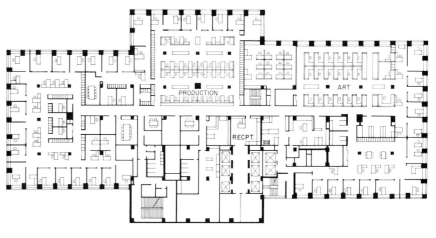

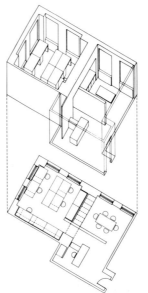

Bill Maris photos

ARCHITECTS' OFFICE: HOBART C. BETTS

Careful, tidy organization of furnishings and equipment, coupled with some simple space-expanding techniques, have produced some very sophisticated quarters for this young New York City firm. Created from a non-descript "L" shaped rental space of about seven hundred square feet, the offices provide a drafting room with six work stations, a reception area, a conference area, and the necessary storage for coats, supplies, reference materials, drawings and records. Sight lines are directed—or blocked—throughout the area by the use of a free-standing center partition, and by carefully placed and lighted pictures. The contractor was H. L. Lazar, Inc.

RCHITECTS' OFFICE: CHARLES E. HUGHES

A 40- by 90-foot floor in a New York City loft building was chosen to accommodate the office of a somewhat unusual, informal "atelier" consisting of several semi-independent professionals. Five-foot high cubicles give the privacy required and a degree of autonomy to each, while allowing light to reach the centrally located portions of the floor. The demountable office partitions are gypsum board on wood studs; lighting fixtures are 18-inch diameter fiberglass globes. Architects Mary T. Hood and Christopher H. L. Owen, and designers John Hughes Hall, Maria Ardena Radoslovich and Joseph Paul D'Urso participated in the joint design.

Joseph W. Molitor photos

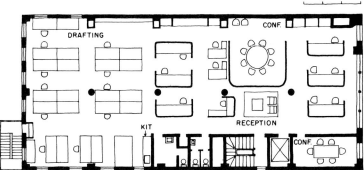

ARCHITECTS' OFFICE: HOBERMAN & WASSERMAN

Differing shapes of two rooms in an old New York building were put to inventive and practical use in this colorful scheme. Private offices, a conference room and a library were accommodated in what was formerly a handball court built on top of the existing roof. A mezzanine to contain the library was introduced to scale down the high ceiling, take best advantage of a skylight, and create space for private offices below. Drafting tables were planned in groups of four to create space for reference surfaces and for impromptu conferences at any desk, and to make best use of the existing 14-foot structural bays of the second, adjacent room. The conference area, shown at left and right, top, is centrally located but gives all the privacy required—openings onto the reception area were windows of the original exterior wall. The contractor was Sweet Construction Corporation.

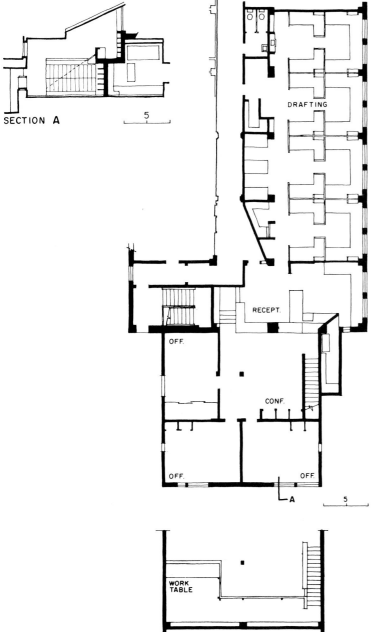

SECTION A   5

DRAFTING

RECEPT.

OFF.

CONF.

OFF.   OFF.

A   5

WORK
TABLE

MEZZANINE

Joseph W. Molitor photos

ARCHITECTS' OFFICE: G. MILTON SMALL & ASSOCIATES

A tree-strewn residential lot near North Carolina State University in Raleigh forms an ideal setting for this little single-occupancy office building. The new building was the result of careful financial studies which led to the decision that constructing rather than leasing space was more economical for the firm, which includes registered personnel for architecture, and mechanical and electrical engineering. The lot is only 69 by 165 feet, but by raising the structure, ample parking and a garden-like approach were provided below the steel-framed and glassed-in offices above. The structural consultant was Ezra Meir and Associates; Frank Walser was contractor.

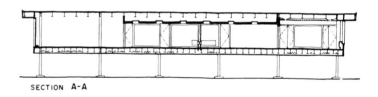

SECTION A-A

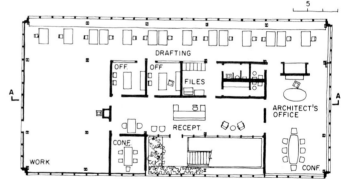

5

DRAFTING

OFF OFF FILES

ARCHITECT'S OFFICE

RECEPT.

WORK CONF. CONF.

A A

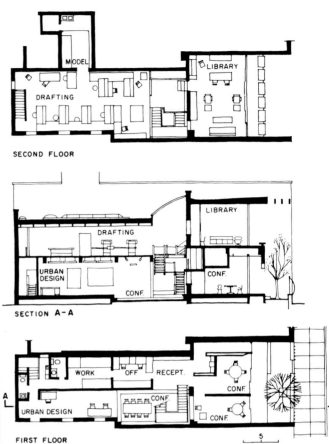

SECOND FLOOR

SECTION A-A

FIRST FLOOR

5

ARCHITECTS' OFFICE: KENNETH W. BROOKS

Deft rehabilitation of a downtown Spokane, Washington, warehouse has created bright, comfortable offices for this firm practicing architecture and urban design. To penetrate spaces with light, the facade was knocked out and replaced with glass, and an arched skylight was placed over the stairwell. It was planned to house 10 to 15 architects and staff and includes such amenities as air conditioning and a fireplace in the library. The old brick was sandblasted and left exposed; new partitions are canvas on gypsum board. Consultants were: Lyerla & Peden (structural); Kendall M. Wood (mechanical); Joseph M. Doyle & Associates (electrical).

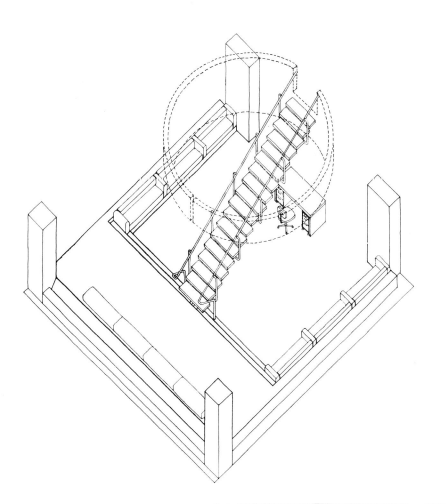

ALCAN CORPORATE OFFICES, Toronto, Canada. Architects: *A. J. Diamond & Barton Myers—A. J. Diamond, Barton Myers & Tony Marsh, design team.* Cost control: *Helyar, Vermeulen, Rae & Mauchan;* mechanical & electrical engineers: *H. H. Angus Associates;* structural engineers: *C. D. Carruthers & Wallace;* general contractors: *McMullen & Warnock Ltd.*

Aluminum-like finishes have been used in many areas of the office, like the planter tubes in the photos above and below, built-in closet doors, and the cube office tables designed by the architects, shown in the photo at right. In the color photo opposite, two coffee tables made from solid aluminum ingots may be seen right and left. The ceilings throughout both floors are those provided by the office building.

The elevator lobby and reception area for the Toronto offices of Aluminum Company of Canada, Ltd., (photo, right and previous page) establish the major visual impact of the offices for a visitor. Neon tubes at the ceiling lead from the elevator space of both floors into the reception area, acting as a strong visual magnet pulling the visitor along. The reception area occupies both floors (see plan and section, page 208) with a spectacularly open, carpeted aluminum stair rising through the center of a full circle cut in the framing of the 21st floor structure.

The building in which these spaces are leased is Mies van der Rohe's 56-story Toronto Dominion Centre (pages (107–116). ALCAN houses about 140 people—including 87 executives—on both floors. A majority of perimeter wall space is thus occupied by private offices, but one of the major objectives of the design was to give secretarial and clerical employees direct outside light, too. The intermittent secretarial bays (see plans, and photo, above left) accomplish this, and eliminate any large, impersonal secretarial pools. The main circulation path around the build-

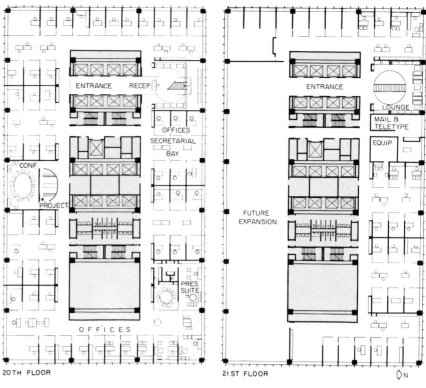

20TH FLOOR

21ST FLOOR

All of the walls of the ALCAN floors in the plans above
are metal studs and gypsum board,
fixed in place. The designers spent extra money
making floor-to-ceiling glass walls
in front, allowing indirect light inside.
Curtains may be drawn in any office for privacy, while
the relatively mullion-free secretarial bays
create a spacious, elegant mood.

Michel Proulx

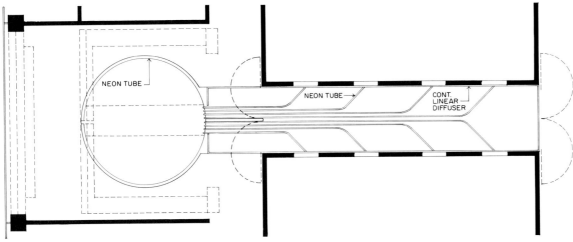

REFLECTED CEILING PLAN—20TH FLOOR

NEON TUBE

NEON TUBE

CONT. LINEAR DIFFUSER

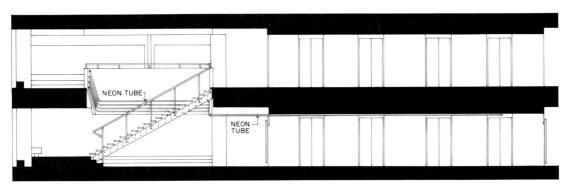

NEON TUBE

NEON TUBE

LONGITUDINAL SECTION

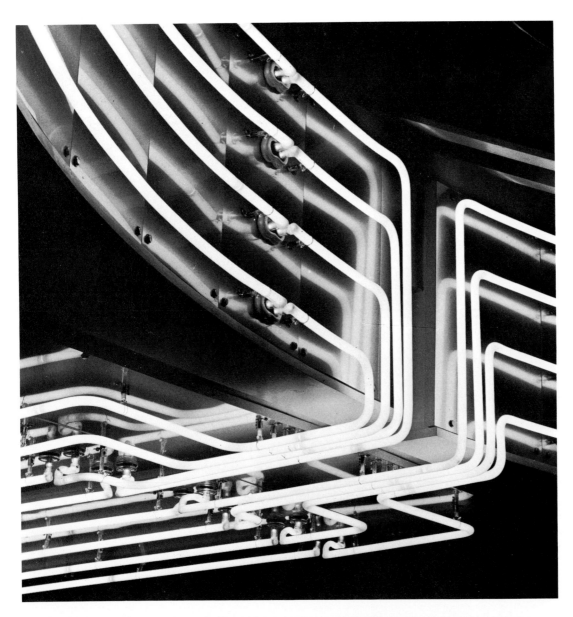

ing's core is more a gallery than a corridor (photo, page 206). It is full seven feet wide, it has exposed incandescent lighting fixtures that cause high contrast and "sparkle" off the silvery glass finishes, and there are built-in filing and coat closets along its length to further mix the use of the space.

The plan and section of the reception and elevator areas (above) help explain the arrangements for neon tubing, so dominant in many of these photographs. One tube leads from each of eight elevator doors, running parallel to each other down the corridor and converging on the aluminum-clad circular passage between floors. At this point the tubes turn 90 degrees vertically, as in the photo at left, and run around the circular opening in both directions. It is a dramatic display of lighting, and a dramatic initial representation of ALCAN's offices.

INDEX